MW01354388

What Am I Doing Here?

A Guide to the Unseen Influence of Your Surroundings

By Adam J. San Juan

First edition 2024

For the pruned and unpruned. Now you know why.

Rusty Ryan

"Off the top of my head, I'd say you're looking at a Boeski, a Jim Brown, a Miss Daisy, two Jethros and a Leon Spinks, not to mention the biggest Ella Fitzgerald ever."[1]

---

[1] In this quote, Rusty Ryan references various code names used in the heist plan from "Ocean's 11," each representing specific roles inspired by cultural figures and references:

- Boeski: Named after Ivan Boesky, a financier known for insider trading, symbolizing the use of insider information.
- Jim Brown: Refers to a staged distraction tactic, named after the iconic American football player, emphasizing the use of diversion.
- Miss Daisy: Represents the use of a SWAT vehicle as a getaway car, alluding to the movie "Driving Miss Daisy" and symbolizing the use of inconspicuous means.
- Two Jethros: Denotes the Malloy brothers, skilled in logistics and mechanics, highlighting the importance of practical skills in the heist.
- Leon Spinks: Indicates a disruption during a boxing match, named after the boxer who famously defeated Muhammad Ali, used here to signify the creation of a major distraction.
- Ella Fitzgerald: Refers to a deceptive tactic involving a looped tape of the heist, inspired by a commercial where Fitzgerald's recorded voice shatters glass, illustrating the illusion of reality.

CONTENTS

Foreword

Is the ability to surround yourself with encouraging and meaningful individuals a special talent, just luck, or is it something we can plan and execute as an individual? Adam San Juan has encapsulated a method of selecting the best persons and environments for you, through his writing in "What Am I Doing Here." Adam gives us a modern approach to navigating relationships and developing a nurturing personal environment. This book faces head on the challenges of relationships and provides helpful strategies to select and develop those relationships that benefit you the most. It also helps us identify those people or places to avoid.

Adam's honesty and ability to use his personal experiences to exhibit the challenges of relationships allows the reader to truly see his perspective in this subject matter. One of the strategies explored includes finding wisdom and identifying foolishness. I found this information important for my own adult children as they navigate the world.

Meeting someone new can be challenging, particularly when in the midst of personal loss. Adam San Juan and I met under one of the worst circumstances, the passing of his mother's husband. It was during this time that I was able to interact with him and his mother as they grieved their loss. I saw Adam's compassion and love for his family and the community. We shared more conversations over the past few years, and I have come to see Adam's passion to share information that is interesting and beneficial in life. He has told me he feels the need to leave his heirs more than cash, he wants to give them wisdom. This book can be used in a variety of settings to increase personal development, both educational settings and professional development. I look forward to sharing this information with others and enjoy the opportunity to share it with you.

My career path has included 30 years developing individuals in the corporate and government setting from interns to program managers to Owner/Operators of franchise companies. I have had the pleasure of seeing individuals develop and prosper. My degrees in Behavioral Science, B.S. and M.S. in Counseling Psychology prepared me well for finding the best in others and growing their potential. Adam San Juan has written a plan for self-development that can also be passed on to others in a team setting. Enjoy the read and pass on the wisdom.

Cynthia White

Henderson, NV

On Purpose

Welcome

Welcome to "What Am I Doing Here?", a guide designed to uncover the subtle yet profound ways in which both personal relationships and our broader surroundings affect our individual development and success. This book provides both theoretical insights and practical, actionable advice to enhance your interpersonal skills and improve your influences in both personal and professional settings.

Understanding the dynamics of our social interactions is essential. These relationships mold our behaviors, influence our decision-making, and shape our worldviews. The quality of these relationships can propel us toward success or hold us back from reaching our potential, underscoring their critical role in our lives.

However, our development is also significantly influenced by the surroundings we inhabit—our workplaces, homes, social circles, and the digital platforms we frequent. This book expands the discussion to examine how these broader factors shape our lives, complementing the interpersonal relationships that form our social foundation.

This guide addresses the need for a “common sense” approach to managing essential relationships and factors effectively. It equips you with tools to refine your social circles and improve your surroundings, offering strategies for nurturing beneficial connections, distancing yourself from toxic influences, and creating environments that inspire and motivate.

With a focus on both the dynamics of effective relationship management and psychology, we cover essential topics such as emotional intelligence, conflict resolution, and the importance of empathy. Case studies are included to help you apply these insights, ensuring that you are equipped to navigate the complexities of modern relationships and contexts.

Furthermore, this book delves into the psychological and emotional dimensions of both relationships and surroundings, explaining their impact on our mental health and life satisfaction. By understanding why some relationships and settings are more fulfilling than others, you will be better prepared to develop a supportive network and an empowering context that aligns with your personal values and goals.

"What Am I Doing Here?" is designed for anyone looking to enhance their interpersonal relationships and improve their quality of life by also reshaping their influences. It encourages a proactive approach in shaping your social landscape and physical contexts, advocating for deliberate and thoughtful choices that prioritize personal growth and happiness.

Through engaging real-life examples throughout the book, this guide offers practical ways to apply these insights directly into your daily life. As you progress, you will gain a comprehensive understanding of the significant role both personal relationships and contextual factors play in shaping your life's trajectory. This book is essential for professionals, entrepreneurs, students, and anyone undergoing major life transitions, aiming to empower them to make transformative shifts in how they view and manage their social circles and environments for a richer, more fulfilling life.

Semi-Spoiler Alert

In the summer of 2012, I embraced the rewarding challenge of coaching my daughter Sydney's 12U travel softball team at a tournament in Orrville, Ohio. Despite logistical hurdles, like last-minute roster changes and initial unfamiliarity among the players, we successfully fostered dynamic team growth.

The third day of the tournament presented an unexpected, yet memorable, bonding opportunity when weather-related delays halted our games. Instead of competing, the team gathered for an impromptu dinner in the hotel lobby. It was during this downtime that the girls creatively decided to construct a "Violations" poster, humorously listing behaviors they deemed unacceptable. This exercise significantly strengthened their sense of community and accountability.

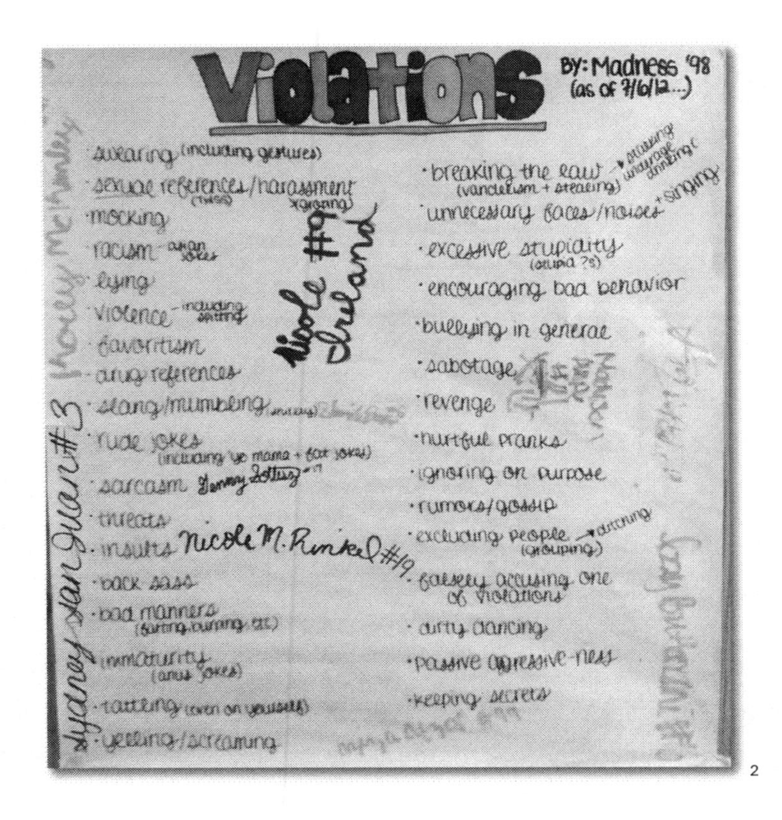

[2]

This poster, encapsulating core values, forged a strong sense of unity and respect among the players. These qualities were evident years later at Sydney's wedding, where her softball teammates,

[2] Here is a complete list of violations:

Swearing, sexual references/harassment, mocking, racism, lying, violence, favoritism, drug references, slang/mumbling, rude jokes, sarcasm, threats, insults, back-sass, bad manners, immaturity, tattling, yelling/screaming, breaking the law, unnecessary faces/noises, excessive stupidity, encouraging bad behavior, bullying, sabotage, revenge, hurtful pranks, ignoring on purpose, rumors/gossip, excluding people, falsely accusing one of violations, dirty dancing, passive aggressiveness, and keeping secrets. Well done, ladies.

including her maid of honor, had met during that pivotal summer. The bonds formed on those playing fields clearly endured well beyond the games.

In the summer of 2014, a similar spirit of camaraderie was evident during a wiffle ball game involving my son Aaron and his friends in our front yard. This gathering of 12 to 15 high school juniors and seniors, both athletes and honor society members, enjoyed a game complete with makeshift bases and unique rules, such as "pegging" the runner with the ball for outs. More than a simple game, this event reinforced relationships that began in their Little League days, now cherished as a regular ritual.

These early friendships, nurtured through shared experiences and mutual respect, were essential as these children matured into successful adults. Over a decade later, individuals from this group, including Aaron, who became a firefighter, and others who became medical professionals and social media influencers, demonstrate the profound impact of nurturing positive early relationships.

The Unseen Influence of Your Surroundings

The people you choose to surround yourself with have a profound impact on your life—shaping your personal growth, your success, and your overall well-being in ways you may not always realize. "The Unseen Influence of Your Surroundings" explores the critical role your relationships play in your journey, and how being intentional about who you walk with can transform your life.

This book is about more than just identifying who is in your life; it's about learning to walk with those who inspire, challenge, and support you. The people you choose to keep close have the power to elevate your thinking, sharpen your skills, and bring out the best in you. It's these relationships that help you grow and thrive, and it's essential to recognize their value.

Equally important is the ability to discern the outcomes of the relationships around you. It's not just about what people say or promise; it's about the results they produce—the fruit of their actions. By paying attention to what your relationships bring into your life, you can make more informed decisions about which connections are truly serving your growth and which ones might be holding you back.

And, as with any garden, growth requires pruning. There are times when you'll need to let go of relationships that no longer serve your best interests, even if it's difficult. This book will guide you in recognizing when it's time to step away from toxic influences or connections that have run their course. Pruning isn't about cutting people out without reason—it's about making space for the right relationships to flourish.

Through real-life examples, you'll discover how to nurture relationships that propel you forward, how to identify when someone's presence is weighing you down, and how to maintain a network of connections that aligns with your values and goals. By walking with the wise, recognizing the impact of your relationships, and making thoughtful choices about who remains in your life, your potential will be unlocked, creating a path to greater fulfillment and success.

Let's begin.

Chapter 1. Walk with the Wise

Jim Rohn

"You are the average of the five people you spend the most time with."[3]

[3] The quote "You are the average of the five people you spend the most time with" is often attributed to motivational speaker Jim Rohn. It reflects the idea that personal development is significantly influenced by the closest social connections. Rohn emphasized that individuals tend to inherit the attitudes, behaviors, and outcomes of those they associate with most closely, suggesting that one's environment plays an indispensable role in shaping their success and life's trajectory.

The Denny's Dilemma Part 1: "A Motley Crew"

This is a true story. The depicted dilemma took place in Waukegan, IL, in 1989. At the request of the morons, the names have been changed. Out of respect for the non-morons, the rest has been told exactly as it occurred.

It was 2:00 AM on a Saturday morning. There were five of us, all misfits. I was just as much a knucklehead as the other four. James, the proclaimed leader of our group, sported a notable swoop-and-drop haircut. Mike was tall, quiet, and carried an Eeyore-like demeanor, trying to emulate James's hairstyle. Heather was disturbingly gorgeous, always smiling, gullible, yet as smart as a fox—imagine a 5'1" Jamie Gertz. Beth, of average looks, carried a maternal aura far beyond her years, reminiscent of Maggie Seaver. We were at Denny's, across the street from Lakehurst Mall, looking like extras from the movie "Less Than Zero."

We had just returned from a house party and were hungry. We settled into a corner booth in the smoking section, the haze of cigarette smoke enveloping us as we perused the menus. James ordered for Heather; Mike chose whatever James ordered; Beth picked the cheapest item on the menu, then proceeded to cut up what James had ordered for Heather into small bites. I opted for the precursor to the now-infamous Moons Over My Hammy - a ham and scrambled egg sandwich with Swiss and American cheeses on grilled artisan bread. Perfect for 2:00 AM! Soon, all the food was consumed. That's when the dilemma began.

The bill arrived, and James made the alpha move of saying he'd cover it. The amount wasn't what caused the peculiar look on his face; it was the realization that he didn't have any money with him. The girls never paid for anything; Mike never said a word; and I had some money, but not enough to cover the bill. According to James, our only options were to dine and dash or to dine and dash. So, that was the plan.

The situation did not feel good, and internally, I questioned, "What am I doing here?"

1.1 The Impact of Your Social Circle

Imagine finding yourself at a crossroad where every person you encounter becomes a signpost, directing your path of personal growth. This analogy goes beyond the traditional "fork in the road[4]" or "road less traveled[5]" metaphors, because each signpost offers a specific sign or message. Your social circle, comprising friends, family, colleagues, and acquaintances, is a diverse mix of experiences, values, and perspectives. These interactions possess the power to fuel your passions, challenge your beliefs, and show new pathways to growth. They can be the driving force propelling you forward or, conversely, transform into roadblocks hindering your progress.

Just as a physical signpost points you in a specific direction, the signposts in your life, embodied by your social circle, offer unique insights and directions that shape your path. Some signposts may guide you towards growth and success, while others may serve as

[4] The "fork in the road" metaphor is often attributed to the Greek philosopher Pythagoras (c. 570 – c. 495 BC). He used this metaphor to describe the choices people make in life, particularly the choice between virtue and vice. In his teachings, Pythagoras emphasized that the decisions we make at these crucial junctures shape our character and determine our future path.

[5] The "road less traveled" metaphor comes from the poem "The Road Not Taken" by Robert Frost, published in 1916. In this poem, the narrator comes across a fork in the road and must choose between two paths. The narrator chooses the path less traveled, which "has made all the difference." This metaphor has come to symbolize the importance of making unconventional or challenging choices in life, often leading to personal growth and unique experiences.

cautionary tales, alerting you to potential pitfalls or negative influences. By recognizing and interpreting these signposts, you can make informed decisions about which paths to follow and which relationships to cultivate.

In this opening section, we delve into six key ways in which your social connections mold your experiences, recognizing that this exploration sheds light on the varied influences that shape our lives. As we examine these influences, keep in mind the significance of each signpost and the specific messages they convey in guiding your personal growth and development.

1. The Role of Social Interactions in Shaping Mindset

Every interaction with another person can subtly influence your thinking and attitude towards life. Positive interactions with individuals who are supportive and encouraging can bolster your confidence and reinforce a growth-oriented mindset. These individuals often provide a sounding board for your ideas and dreams, offering constructive feedback and essential encouragement.

Conversely, regular exposure to negative or toxic individuals can instill doubt and pessimism. Such interactions may lead to a mindset that hesitates rather than embraces challenges, which can stymie personal and professional growth. The attitudes and behaviors of those around us can reinforce our worst fears about failure or embolden our aspirations.

2. Influence on Habits and Routines

The habits and routines we develop are often reflections of the people we surround ourselves with. For instance, if your social circle prioritizes health and fitness, you are more likely to adopt similar habits. If your peers value continuous learning and intellectual engagement, you might find yourself participating in educational activities and discussions more frequently.

The opposite is also true; spending time with individuals who have detrimental habits can lead to adopting those same patterns. This could include anything from unhealthy eating and sedentary lifestyles to more severe issues like substance abuse. The power of social influence on our daily practices and long-term health can be significant.

3. Decision-Making Processes

Your social circle also impacts how you make decisions, both minor and major. Being surrounded by a diverse group of thoughtful, insightful individuals can provide you with a range of perspectives that enhance your ability to weigh different options and make well-informed choices. These individuals can challenge your assumptions, push you to think differently, and help you see possibilities you might not have considered on your own.

In contrast, a homogeneous group that rarely challenges your viewpoints or offers new insights can limit your decision-making scope. This can result in choices that are safe and unchallenging, potentially keeping you from making bold moves that could lead to significant personal growth.

4. Emotional and Psychological Support

A supportive social circle offers emotional sustenance and psychological strength, helping you navigate the ups and downs of life. During periods of stress, uncertainty, or change, having a network of compassionate and understanding individuals can make a substantial difference in your ability to cope and adapt.

The absence of such support can leave you vulnerable to stress and anxiety, potentially impacting your mental health and overall well-being. The emotional echo chamber of a supportive network acts not only as a cushion during tough times but also as a celebratory force during moments of success and joy.

5. Opening Doors to Opportunities

The relationships you cultivate can open doors to new opportunities that you might not have access to on your own. This includes career opportunities, new ventures, collaborations, and introductions to influential or knowledgeable individuals. Your social circle can act as a bridge to experiences and networks that propel you towards personal and professional milestones.

However, a limited or negatively influential social circle might close off these pathways, keeping you within a bubble that neither challenges nor advances your capabilities or career prospects.

6. Long-Term Impact on Personal Development

The long-term impact of your social circle on your personal development is undeniable. The beliefs, behaviors, and attitudes cultivated through your relationships can define the trajectory of your life. The choice of who you allow into your inner circle should be made with care, considering not only what you can gain from the relationship but also what you can offer. Mutual growth and support ensure that the benefits are reciprocal, fostering an environment where all parties are encouraged to thrive.

From Influence to Insight

As we reflect on the profound impact our social circles have on our personal development, it becomes essential to advance our understanding of how wisdom and foolishness play out in our relationships. Transitioning from the broad influence of our interactions, we delve deeper into the nuanced dynamics that dictate the quality of these relationships. This next section builds on the understanding that, while our environment shapes us, the essence of our relationships hinges on the wisdom or foolishness they embody. We move from recognizing the general influence of our social interactions to specifically identifying and fostering relationships that are not only supportive but also enriching. In doing so, we aim to distinguish those connections that contribute positively to our growth from those that may hinder it, guiding you through a strategic approach to improve and maintain relationships that are rooted in wisdom, mutual respect, and personal development.

1.2 Defining Wisdom and Foolishness

Within the intricate web of personal development, the distinctions between wisdom and foolishness take center stage, particularly in our relationships. These fundamental concepts not only shape our interactions but also serve as guiding lights on our journey of growth. As we delve into the six key concepts ahead, we unravel the critical nuances that delineate relationships marked by wisdom from those colored by foolishness. Understanding these concepts is not just insightful; it's imperative for navigating the complexities of our social connections and fostering transformative growth.

1. Discernment and Personal Growth

Wisdom: Wisdom in relationships is exemplified by discernment, a deep commitment to personal and mutual growth, and the strategic selection of companions who positively influence one's emotional and intellectual development. Wise individuals not only seek support but also challenge and shared values, fostering a nurturing environment that propels both parties toward their best selves.

Foolishness: Conversely, foolishness is characterized by a glaring lack of discernment, with a focus on short-term gratification that often comes at the expense of long-term stability and well-being. These relationships prioritize immediate pleasure or superficial validation, which stifles growth and may promote harmful behaviors or complacency.

2. Learning and Openness to New Ideas

Wisdom: Wise individuals are committed to lifelong learning and self-improvement, engaging with mentors and peers who possess admirable qualities and challenge them to expand their horizons. They value diverse viewpoints and are committed to incorporating new insights into their personal ethos.

Foolishness: In contrast, foolishness manifests as a stubborn resistance to new perspectives, resulting in a preference for echo chambers that reinforce unchallenged, often limiting beliefs. This environment encourages a closed mindset, leading to the rejection of constructive criticism and missed opportunities for growth.

3. Setting Healthy Boundaries

Wisdom: Wise individuals understand the critical importance of setting and respecting healthy boundaries to protect their emotional health and maintain a balanced life. They consciously choose relationships that respect these boundaries, fostering environments of mutual respect and personal well-being.

Foolishness: Conversely, foolish behavior often includes the neglect of personal boundaries, leading to relationships that are emotionally draining and unbalanced. This neglect can result in significant emotional exhaustion and hinder one's ability to function effectively in other areas of life.

4. Authenticity and Vulnerability

Wisdom: Embracing authenticity and vulnerability, wise individuals foster relationships that are built on trust and open communication. They are confident in expressing their true selves, which invites deeper and more meaningful interactions, enhancing relational satisfaction and mutual growth.

Foolishness: On the flip side, foolishness is often characterized by superficiality and the hiding behind social masks, which prevents the formation of deep and meaningful relationships. This lack of genuine connection can lead to isolation and dissatisfaction within relationships.

5. Proactivity in Addressing Conflicts

Wisdom: Wise individuals approach conflicts proactively, with a focus on open dialogue and resolution that prioritizes the health of the relationship. They use conflicts as opportunities for insight, strengthening bonds and fostering deeper understanding.

Foolishness: Conversely, foolishness in relationships includes avoiding necessary confrontations and letting unresolved issues fester, which can erode trust and weaken bonds, ultimately leading to the deterioration of the relationship.

6. Flexibility and Adaptation

Wisdom: Wise individuals acknowledge the dynamic nature of relationships and are prepared to adapt to changing circumstances. They view adaptability as an essential component of a healthy relationship, facilitating growth and resilience.

Foolishness: In contrast, foolishness often manifests as rigidity and inflexibility, refusing to adapt to new situations or reconsider outdated behaviors, which can lead to stagnation and dissatisfaction within relationships.

Navigating from Insight to Implementation

As we wrap up our study of discerning wisdom and foolishness in relationships, it's essential to shift from theoretical understanding to practical application. Recognizing the attributes of wisdom and foolishness provides a foundational framework; however, the real challenge lies in actively integrating this knowledge into our daily interactions and choices. This next section builds upon our insights by offering concrete strategies for seeking out and nurturing relationships with wise individuals. By applying these strategies, we can ensure that our social circle not only reflects our values but actively contributes to our personal and professional growth. Through intentional efforts to surround ourselves with wise and supportive individuals, we enhance our capacity for self-actualization and navigate life's challenges with greater resilience and insight.

1.3 Seeking Out the Wise

For personal growth and self-actualization, surrounding yourself with wise individuals is essential. These relationships, brimming with guidance, unwavering support, and boundless inspiration, serve as an invaluable compass, steering you through life's complexities and unveiling hidden opportunities. Cultivating such profound connections demands a deliberate and strategic approach. In this section, we present a comprehensive roadmap for discovering and nurturing bonds with wise mentors, propelling your personal and professional evolution. There are ten key strategies for fostering these transformative connections that are covered in this guide, but it's worth noting that there are other possible avenues beyond these pages. The realm of relationship-building offers myriad paths, each capable of contributing significantly to your continual growth and ultimate success.

1. Defining Wisdom

Begin by defining what wisdom means to you. Reflect on the qualities you admire in others—whether that's emotional intelligence, practical knowledge, resilience, a strong moral compass, or the ability to inspire others. Then, determine how these traits align with your personal values and aspirations. Understanding what constitutes wisdom for you will help you identify and attract those who embody these traits, aiding in the development of meaningful mentorships and peer relationships that can significantly influence your personal growth.

2. Expanding Your Circle

Actively seek out and participate in events and gatherings that resonate with your interests, such as workshops, seminars, or conferences. These venues are prime opportunities to meet like-minded individuals who are also committed to personal growth. Engage openly, share your experiences, and participate in discussions to foster potential mentorships and friendships that could be pivotal in your path to growth.

3. Leveraging Mentorship

Identify potential mentors who demonstrate the wisdom you seek. Approach them with respect and clarity about your interest in their experiences and insights, clearly communicating your specific goals. While establishing and maintaining these relationships requires effort, the guidance gained are often invaluable. Effective mentorship involves a reciprocal exchange of ideas and experiences, enriching both parties involved.

4. Nurturing Existing Relationships

Consistently engage with those who inspire and challenge you. Regular interactions, whether through scheduled meetings, calls, or informal gatherings, can deepen these relationships. Approach these interactions with an openness to listen and share, fostering an environment of mutual growth and respect.

5. Maintaining Autonomy

While it is beneficial to seek advice, remember that you are the principal architect of your life. Use the wisdom you acquire to inform and enhance your decisions, not dictate them. Maintaining autonomy and trusting your judgment are essential for integrating external advice effectively while staying true to your own values and goals.

6. Commitment to Lifelong Learning

Pursue knowledge and new experiences relentlessly to expand your worldview. This commitment not only enriches your personal life but also makes you a more compelling and attractive companion in wise relationships. Lifelong learning keeps your mind open and eager to absorb new ideas, which is essential for maintaining relationships.

7. Sharing Your Wisdom

As you gather knowledge and experience, actively share your insights with others. Providing support not only enriches the lives of those around you but also enhances your relationships and fosters a positive community of mutual growth. This exchange encourages a culture where wisdom circulates freely, benefiting everyone involved.

8. Embracing Authenticity and Diversity

Prioritize authenticity and embrace vulnerability in your interactions. Genuine relationships require openness and trust, which are foundational for meaningful connections. Actively seek diverse perspectives to broaden your understanding of the world. Embracing a variety of viewpoints enriches your personal growth process, helping you develop a comprehensive perspective on life.

9. Being Patient and Persistent

Understand that building meaningful relationships takes time and patience. Embrace the process. Recognize that not every connection will perfectly fit or fulfill all expectations. Remain open to learning from each interaction and celebrate the small victories along the way. Persistence in nurturing these relationships will eventually lead to a robust network of wise individuals who support and enrich your life.

10. Reassessing Relationships

As you grow and evolve, so too should your relationships. Regularly assess your social circle to ensure it remains aligned with your values and continues to support your growth. Be prepared to make difficult decisions. Don't be afraid to let go of connections that no longer serve you and let in the ones that do. This ongoing process of reassessment is critical to keeping your relationships relevant and supportive as you navigate different stages of your life.

From Cultivation to Caution

As we transition from exploring strategies to cultivate relationships with wise individuals, it becomes imperative to reflect on the inverse: the consequences of engaging with detrimental influences. The previous section equipped us with tools to identify and nurture beneficial connections. Now, we shift our focus to the hazards of associating with those who may impede our growth. This segment highlights the significance of vigilance and proactive management in our social interactions. It's true that negative relationships can erode our well-being and impede our paths to success. By understanding these pitfalls, we prepare ourselves to make informed decisions about who we allow into our lives, ensuring our circle remains a source of support and positive influence.

1.4 Associating with Fools

The company you keep profoundly influences your personal growth, well-being, and overall success. Surrounding yourself with wise individuals can create an environment that uplifts and inspires you. Doors to new possibilities will open, empowering you to reach your full potential. Conversely, associating with foolish or negative influences can significantly hinder your progress and obstruct your path to success. In this section, there are six specific consequences of negative associations. Each consequence sheds light on the potential negative impacts on your life resulting from the influences you choose to accept. These consequences are among the most common, but it's crucial to note that other negative outcomes may also arise, depending on the nature of the negative influences in your life.

1. The Erosion of Positivity

One of the most profound impacts of maintaining negative associations is the gradual erosion of your own positive mindset and habits. Regular exposure to pessimistic attitudes or toxic behaviors can make you susceptible to adopting these same destructive patterns. This subtle and often unnoticed shift can gradually undermine your motivation, self-belief, and determination, making it increasingly challenging to maintain a growth-oriented mindset.

2. Emotional Consequences

Consider the emotional toll that comes from spending time with individuals who constantly complain, criticize, or engage in gossip. Their pervasive negative energy acts like a toxic vapor that can seep into our thoughts and emotions, seeping into your thoughts and emotions, leading to increased stress, anxiety, and self-doubt. Over time, you might find yourself becoming more cynical and judgmental. Don't focus on the negatives of life, rather recognize opportunities for growth and improvement.

3. Hindrance to Personal Aspirations

Foolish or negative influences can actively discourage you from pursuing your goals. These individuals may belittle your aspirations or question your abilities, which can make you second-guess yourself and possibly abandon your ambitions. This type of environment can trap you within the confines of their self-imposed limitations.

4. Risk of Destructive Behaviors

Another significant concern is the potential for adopting destructive behaviors or making poor decisions. Spending time with individuals who prioritize instant gratification, engage in risky activities, or disregard the consequences of their actions can influence you to follow suit. The normalization of unhealthy habits within your social circle can tempt you to engage in similar behaviors, which may lead to long-lasting consequences such as damaged relationships or even legal troubles.

5. Stagnation in Growth

Negative associations can restrict your exposure to new ideas, perspectives, and opportunities for growth. When you are surrounded by individuals who are content with mediocrity, resist change, or have a narrow worldview, you risk stagnating in your personal and professional development. This stagnation can hinder your ability to excel in your career or pursue your entrepreneurial goals, severely limiting your potential for success.

6. Impact on Reputation

The people you associate with can also reflect poorly on your character and judgment. Being seen with individuals known for dishonesty or unethical behavior can tarnish your reputation. You don't want to miss out on personal or professional opportunities. Damage to your reputation is often subtle and gradual, so it's essential to assess your social circle regularly and make conscious choices about the individuals you allow into your life.

Actively seeking out positive influences can broaden your horizons and offer fresh perspectives and valuable insights essential for personal growth. These influencers not only foster skill development but also unveil new opportunities, empowering you to achieve greater fulfillment. Conversely, if negative influences surround you, establish clear boundaries. Connect with individuals who embody the qualities you admire. Create a supportive network that propels your personal evolution.

Having explored the consequences of associating with foolish or negative influences, we understand how critical it is to surround ourselves with positive and constructive relationships. This awareness not only helps us avoid the pitfalls of negative associations but also reinforces the value of nurturing beneficial connections.

In the next section, we will shift our focus to the profound impact that "Walking with the Wise" has on shaping industries through strategic collaborations and influential partnerships.

1.5 Case Studies

The Good

Steve Jobs and Steve Wozniak

Steve Jobs and Steve Wozniak co-founded Apple Inc. in 1976, a partnership that would redefine the technology landscape. Wozniak, the technical wizard, and Jobs, the visionary marketer, introduced the Apple I computer at a local computer club, an event marking the dawn of the personal computer era. This was followed by the Apple II, which became a mass-market success due to its more user-friendly interface and appealing design. Their collaborative efforts did not just innovate product design and user experience; they set the foundation for future Apple products and laid the groundwork for personal computing as a fundamental part of modern life. The ethos of combining aesthetics with functionality, driven by their partnership, remains a cornerstone of Apple's corporate identity.

Elon Musk and Nikola Tesla

Elon Musk's ventures, particularly Tesla Motors, draw significant inspiration from Nikola Tesla, the Serbian-American inventor known for his contributions to the development of electricity and energy systems. Founded in 2003 and named after Nikola Tesla, Tesla, Inc. epitomizes the spirit of Tesla's innovative work, particularly through its development of electric vehicles and renewable energy solutions. Musk's broader portfolio, including SpaceX, also reflects Tesla's vision of bold, scientific advancements. Musk's adoption of Tesla's name and legacy underscores a commitment to major technological innovations that challenge traditional industries, from automotive to aerospace.

Mark Zuckerberg and WhatsApp Founders (Jan Koum and Brian Acton)

In 2014, Facebook acquired WhatsApp for approximately $19 billion, a landmark deal in the tech world led by Facebook's CEO, Mark Zuckerberg. Founders Jan Koum and Brian Acton developed WhatsApp with a focus on privacy and minimalistic design, which attracted hundreds of millions of users worldwide. Under Facebook, WhatsApp has maintained its user-centric approach while integrating with Facebook's infrastructure, enhancing global communication accessibility. This acquisition highlights the strategic vision of Zuckerberg to expand Facebook's messaging capabilities, recognizing the growing importance of instant, secure communication in the digital age, and shaping how people connect across the globe.

Richard Branson and Nelson Mandela

Despite their differing paths—Richard Branson, a British entrepreneur, and Nelson Mandela, South Africa's first black president and a global icon of peace—their collaborations on social and humanitarian issues highlight the power of cross-sector partnerships. Together, they worked on projects aimed at social healing and educational programs through organizations like The Elders and Virgin Unite. Their joint initiatives often focused on global peace, health, and community development, demonstrating the impact influential figures can have when they unite around shared humanitarian goals. This partnership transcended cultural and economic boundaries, setting a precedent for future collaborations across diverse fields.

NASA and LEGO

The partnership between NASA and LEGO is a stellar example of how educational tools can inspire future generations in science, technology, engineering, and mathematics (STEM). This collaboration, which began in the late 1990s and expanded over the years, leverages LEGO's appeal to foster interest and education in space exploration. Through meticulously-designed LEGO sets that replicate NASA's spacecraft and missions, alongside educational materials and events, this partnership enriches STEM education by making it engaging and accessible to children worldwide. The initiative not only educates but also sparks imagination and curiosity about space, encouraging a new generation of scientists, engineers, and explorers.

The Bad and The Ugly

Billy McFarland

The founder of the Fyre Festival, Billy McFarland, orchestrated what was promoted as an ultra-luxurious music festival on a private island in 2017. Instead, attendees found themselves stranded with inadequate food, shelter, and security. McFarland's fraudulent misrepresentations and financial improprieties led to a six-year prison sentence and highlighted the dangers of deceptive promotional practices in the entertainment industry.

The FIFA Corruption Scandal

Exposed in 2015, this scandal revealed extensive corruption within FIFA, with several senior officials indicted on charges including racketeering, wire fraud, and money laundering. The allegations included bribery related to the awarding of hosting rights for the World Cup and other major FIFA tournaments, undermining the credibility of international soccer governance. The fallout was extensive, resulting in resignations, arrests, and ongoing scrutiny of international sports administration practices.

Sumo Wrestling Match-Fixing Scandal

This scandal emerged in 2011 when evidence surfaced that numerous matches in the deeply traditional and culturally significant sport of sumo wrestling in Japan had been fixed.

Investigations revealed that several wrestlers and referees were involved, leading to retirements and lifetime bans. The scandal tarnished the sport's honorable image, prompting reforms aimed at restoring integrity and public confidence.

Ken Lay and Jeffrey Skilling

The collapse of Enron, under the leadership of Ken Lay and Jeffrey Skilling, became one of the most infamous corporate frauds when it unraveled in 2001. As CEO and COO, respectively, Lay and Skilling were central figures in using accounting loopholes and special purpose entities to hide massive debt and inflate the company's financial health. This deception not only led to the bankruptcy of Enron but also resulted in thousands of employees losing their jobs and life savings, while shaking trust in corporate governance and prompting new regulations like the Sarbanes-Oxley Act.

The Chicago Black Sox

In one of the earliest major scandals in American sports, eight members of the Chicago White Sox conspired to throw the 1919 World Series in exchange for money from gamblers. The plot's discovery led to the players, including star "Shoeless" Joe Jackson, being banned for life from baseball, casting a permanent shadow over their careers and altering the course of the sport. The scandal not only disillusioned fans but also brought about significant changes in how Major League Baseball was governed.

"The Dinner Test"

Imagine entering a bustling restaurant with someone important to you--perhaps a spouse, a client, your boss, or family members ranging from parents to grandparents. As you look around, you notice two distinct tables, each beckoning you to join them.

At the Table of Integrity sit luminaries and pioneers: Steve Jobs and Steve Wozniak, Elon Musk inspired by Nikola Tesla, Mark Zuckerberg with WhatsApp founders Jan Koum and Brian Acton, Richard Branson alongside Nelson Mandela, and representatives from NASA and LEGO. This table epitomizes innovation, leadership, and positive societal impact.

The second table hosts a contrasting group, the Table of Controversy: Billy McFarland, key figures from the FIFA Corruption Scandal, participants in the Sumo Wrestling Match-Fixing Scandal, Ken Lay and Jeffrey Skilling of Enron, and members of the Chicago Black Sox. This assembly symbolizes cautionary tales of ambition corrupted by ethical lapses and severe misjudgments.

As representatives from both tables enthusiastically invite you and your companion to join them, consider not just which table you would choose but why you would make that choice. What values and potential outcomes influence your decision? This exercise isn't just about choosing a seat; it's a moment to reflect on the significant impact that the company we keep has on our personal and professional lives.

Now, imagine if behind each table were two more tables of ten that included the following people. Does that confirm where you would like to sit or make it more confusing?

Table of Integrity Additions:

- Condoleezza Rice: Known for her diplomatic expertise and commitment to global peace.
- Dalai Lama: Revered spiritual leader promoting compassion and non-violence.
- J.R.R. Tolkien: Renowned author celebrated for his imaginative storytelling and moral themes.
- Jeff Bezos: Innovator who transformed e-commerce while emphasizing customer satisfaction.
- Margaret Thatcher: Influential political leader advocating for economic and individual freedom.
- Martin Luther King Jr.: Civil rights icon championing equality and nonviolent activism.
- Michael Jordan: Legendary athlete known for his work ethic, competitiveness, and philanthropy.
- Mother Teresa: Saintly figure dedicated to serving the poor and marginalized.

- Tim Cook: Ethical leader at Apple, emphasizing social responsibility and innovation.
- Winston Churchill: Respected statesman known for his leadership during challenging times.

Table of Controversy Additions:

- Al Franken: Involved in political controversies and allegations of misconduct.
- Andrew Cuomo: Faced scandals related to leadership and workplace conduct.
- Anthony Weiner: Involved in scandals related to inappropriate online behavior.
- Colin Kaepernick: Controversial figure due to his protests against racial injustice.
- Elizabeth Holmes: Involved in legal issues related to fraud and deception in business.
- Harvey Weinstein: A former Hollywood mogul, was convicted of sexual misconduct, becoming a symbol of the #MeToo movement and abuse of power.
- James Comey: Controversial for his actions and decisions while serving as FBI director.
- Keith Olbermann: Known for controversial statements and opinions in media.
- Kevin Spacey: Involved in scandals related to allegations of misconduct and abuse.

- Tonya Harding: Associated with controversies in figure skating, including a notorious scandal.

Consider how the inclusion of these additional figures may further clarify or complicate your decision on where to sit, and what deeper insights it may offer into your values and ethical considerations.

The Devil's Advocate

Before you make your final decision, let's consider another perspective: Is it really so black and white? The Table of Integrity may seem like the obvious choice, filled with leaders known for their innovation, compassion, and positive impact. But what about those at the Table of Controversy? Could spending time with individuals who have faced scandal or controversy offer valuable lessons?

It might be intriguing to sit with them for a little while—to hear their stories, understand the motivations behind their decisions, and gain insight into how their downfalls unfolded. There's value in learning from their mistakes, in seeing firsthand how ambition, misjudgment, or ethical lapses can lead to dramatic consequences. Their experiences serve as powerful warnings, highlighting the fragile balance between success and failure.

However, while their stories may be insightful, these individuals likely wouldn't be part of your core circle. Engaging with them might offer a fresh perspective or valuable cautionary lessons, but when it comes to the *relationships* that shape your long-term growth and success, you want people whose values align with yours.

That said, it's important to recognize that the decision to place someone at the Table of Integrity or the Table of Controversy is entirely subjective. The fact that I've categorized these individuals based on what they're known for—and how I chose to summarize their contributions—says as much about me and my values as it does about them. You, as the reader, might not agree with my choices, and that's okay. But in reading this, you're already forming a picture of who I am and what I prioritize.

The devil's advocate asks: What might you learn from briefly sitting at the table of controversy, and how would it remind you of the importance of maintaining a core circle that reflects your own values and long-term aspirations? At the same time, how do my selections and reflections influence your understanding of me and, perhaps, your own values?

1.6 Walk with the Wise: Five Key Takeaways

1. Your Social Circle Shapes Your Growth

   The influence of your social circle is profound and far-reaching, affecting not only your immediate mood and behaviors but also your long-term aspirations and abilities. Engaging with positive, inspiring individuals can significantly accelerate your growth, encouraging you to reach higher and achieve more. Conversely, negative relationships can sap your energy and distract you from your goals, proving that the company you keep is integral to your success.

2. Discernment is Essential

   Effective discernment in choosing your companions is essential. This involves more than recognizing who brings joy and who brings stress; it requires a thoughtful analysis of how each relationship aligns with your long-term goals and values. Be prepared to make tough decisions to sever ties with those who consistently drain your energy or detract from your growth and cherish those who uplift and challenge you.

3. Personal Growth is a Collaborative Process

Personal development is significantly enhanced by the insights and encouragement of others. While self-growth starts internally, it is powerfully driven by external collaborations. Surround yourself with mentors, peers, and supporters who not only share your aspirations but also push you towards new challenges and offer feedback that fosters your growth.

4. Embrace Wisdom, Avoid Foolishness

Cultivating wisdom within your relationships means actively seeking out and nurturing connections with individuals who demonstrate maturity, insight, and a constructive approach to life. This includes valuing long-term over short-term gains, embracing changes that promote growth, and maintaining open, honest communication. Actively avoid relationships characterized by shortsightedness, superficiality, and negativity, which can trap you in cycles of unproductive behavior.

5. Nurture Your Inner Circle

Building and maintaining a supportive inner circle is an ongoing process that demands deliberate effort and continuous reassessment. As you grow and your needs evolve, so too should your relationships. Regularly reflect on the dynamics of your interactions, being ready to introduce new, enriching connections and phase out those that no longer serve your best interests. This dynamic approach ensures that your social environment remains aligned with your personal and professional evolution, providing a foundation of support that adapts to your changing life.

1.7 Walk with the Wise: Ten Key Questions

1. How do the five closest people in your life influence your thoughts and actions—are they positive, neutral, or negative?
2. Can you identify a relationship in your life that exemplifies wisdom or foolishness? How do these relationships affect your decisions?
3. What actions have you taken to seek and nurture relationships with wise individuals, and how have these affected your growth?
4. Which case study discussed resonates most with you, and why? How can you apply the lessons from that story to your life?
5. What changes have you noticed in yourself since evaluating your social circle based on wisdom and foolishness?
6. Are there any relationships you need to reevaluate or distance yourself from based on insights from this section?
7. How often do you assess the impact of your social circle on your personal and professional goals?

8. What are the major challenges in forming and maintaining wise relationships, and how can you overcome them?
9. What criteria will you use moving forward to decide whether to cultivate or curtail a relationship based on the concepts discussed in this section?
10. If faced with the choice between the two tables at "The Dinner Test," one symbolizing innovators and leaders in positive societal impact, and the other reflecting cautionary tales of ambition overshadowed by ethical lapses and misjudgments, which table would you choose? Justify your decision, taking into account the values, potential outcomes, and ethical implications associated with your choice.

Navigating from Wisdom to Outcomes

Having explored the profound influence of our social circles in "Walk with the Wise," where we talked about how our relationships can either bolster or stifle our personal and professional growth, we now transition into a deeper investigation in "Recognizing the Fruit." This next chapter builds on the foundation laid previously by focusing on the tangible outcomes of our interactions. It offers practical tools for assessing the character and values of those around us, identifying red flags in relationships, and evaluating the impact these relationships have on our own life trajectory. By learning to discern the real effects of our social engagements, we empower ourselves to make informed decisions about who we let into our inner circle, ensuring that our associations reflect our values and support our ambitions.

Chapter 2. Recognizing the Fruit

Harvey Dent

"You either die a hero, or you live long enough to see yourself become the villain."[6]

[6] In The Dark Knight, Harvey Dent's quote, "You either die a hero, or you live long enough to see yourself become the villain," reflects the film's examination of moral dilemmas and the fragility of heroism. This line, spoken by Dent, encapsulates his transformation and the broader theme that even the most principled individuals can become corrupted or undergo drastic changes over time under certain circumstances. The quote serves as a cautionary statement about the potential for shifts in one's character and values, especially when confronted with prolonged adversity or temptation.

The Denny’s Dilemma Part 2: "Should I Stay or Should I Go"

The plan went off without a hitch. I shouldn’t have been so surprised. Denny's is always crowded at 2:00 AM on a Saturday night. Along with the house parties, there were other local hotspots like the Greenleaf Inn just around the corner in Park City and Blue Suede Shoes on Old 41. In short, the freaks came out at night, and this helped.

For me, the obvious dilemma wasn’t “do we dine and ditch?” It was “do I dine and ditch?” Is this in my character? What happens if I get caught? Is it worth it for these “friends”? What happens if I chicken out and run? And even if we were successful, do we brag about this? Is this even worth bragging about? What does this say about us? About me? "Ha, ha, we ripped off Denny's!" And could I ever show my face at Denny's again? The walk to the getaway car seemed like it was in slow motion. My guess is that the walk was all about 100 feet, yet it felt like 100 yards! So much was going on in my head, but I chose to fall in line, as planned.

We were all in the car, girls in the front, boys in the back. Oh, and Robert Smith. The Cure was playing on the radio, 102.3 WXLC. And that's all you heard.

I was dropped off first because I lived the closest. Some version of a salutation was said--I can't remember exactly--then off went the Cavalier of criminals. I remember being in my room, not exactly sure what to think or do. I couldn't sleep, 3:30 AM, 4:30 AM. I had to do something. Then, I just did it. After I changed outfits into something more preppy (all black in Z Cavaricci's doesn't exude innocence), I hopped in my car, drove to the nearest cash station, withdrew $100, and made my way back to the scene of the crime with a pocket full of loot and a mind full of guilt. I was going to make this right.

2.1 Assessing Character and Values

Choosing who we surround ourselves with profoundly influences our personal growth and self-actualization. The company we keep can either nurture our potential or hinder our progress, emphasizing the importance of discernment in managing our relationships. This section aims to equip you with five practical methods to accurately assess the character and values of those in your inner circle, ensuring that your relationships foster your development rather than impede it.

1. Observing Actions Over Words

At the heart of discernment lies the ability to accurately evaluate the character and values of individuals in our inner circle. Prioritizing observation of actions over words is essential, as actions often reveal more about a person's true character than their statements. This observation becomes particularly telling during times of adversity or when individuals interact with others from whom they have nothing to gain. How a person handles challenges, treats their peers, and maintains integrity in various settings offers profound insights into their genuine nature. The forthcoming sections will expand further on the implications of these observations.

2. Assessing Values in Action

It's essential to observe how people behave under pressure and how they treat others, especially those who can offer them no direct benefits. These behaviors are telling indicators of a person's true character. Assessing someone's values in action involves noting whether they consistently demonstrate honesty, loyalty, and openness to growth. Conversely, observe if they exhibit deceit, selfishness, or a tendency to resist change. This evaluation helps identify the core values that drive their decisions and interactions, providing a clearer picture of their moral compass.

3. Consistency and Integrity

Evaluating how individuals respond to adversity, manage stress, and treat people in less-privileged positions can reveal a lot about their capacity for empathy, resilience, and integrity. For example, observe whether they approach difficult situations with a positive, solution-oriented attitude or if they become overwhelmed and withdraw. Consistency in these behaviors across different situations is a critical indicator of a person's true integrity and authenticity. Such consistency shows that they do not merely perform virtues when convenient but live by them.

4. Setting Boundaries

As you continue to evaluate the people around you, trust your instincts about whom to trust and whom to maintain distance from. It is important to set boundaries with individuals who consistently exhibit behaviors that are misaligned with your values or that negatively impact your emotional well-being. Conversely, foster closer relationships with those who positively influence your growth and reflect the values you admire. Setting these boundaries is essential for maintaining a healthy and supportive social environment.

5. Ongoing Evaluation

It's an ongoing process to assess the character and values of the people around you. As you grow and evolve, so too should your understanding of how relationships fit into your life. Regular reflection and reassessment of connections ensure that they continue to support your needs and align with your evolving values. Be willing to adjust your inner circle as necessary to ensure you are surrounded by a network that genuinely supports your growth and well-being.

The quality of your relationships significantly impacts your personal and professional development. By thoughtfully choosing and maintaining connections with individuals who reflect the character and values you respect, you build a strong foundation for your own growth and success.

From Words to Actions: Unveiling True Character

Having explored practical methods to assess the character and values of those around us, we now shift our focus to a more granular level: the significance of actions over words. This transition underscores the evolution from evaluating broad personal traits to understanding how these characteristics manifest in everyday behaviors. In the next section, we will talk about how consistent actions rather than mere words truly outline a person's integrity and authenticity, emphasizing the practical application of our assessments in real-world interactions. This critical perspective enables us to navigate our relationships more wisely, ensuring that we surround ourselves with individuals whose actions consistently reflect their spoken values and ethical standards.

2.2 Actions Over Words

In understanding human connections, it is clear that while words can inspire or deceive, true character is consistently revealed through actions. This realization is pivotal as we navigate our interactions, requiring that eloquent words be backed by consistent actions to genuinely reflect a person's integrity and authenticity.

Consider a colleague who impresses with persuasive promises yet repeatedly fails to deliver. This gap between words and actions raises questions about their reliability. Similarly, a friend may profess loyalty but fails to support you in challenging times, revealing their true priorities. These discrepancies are clear indicators of an individual's reliability and ethical stance.

True integrity is demonstrated by those who align their actions with their principles consistently and unassumingly. Such individuals earn trust and respect not through grand gestures but through their quiet, steadfast behaviors. Actions, not words, are the true measure of a person's character.

This principle is fundamental not only in evaluating others but also in personal growth. Declarations about self-improvement are only as credible as the actions that follow. For example, advocating for healthy living while indulging in unhealthy habits shows a disconnect between stated values and actual behaviors.

The ability to observe actions is indispensable in our relationships and personal development. Consistent behavior, especially in adversity, offers real insights into a person's character, guiding us towards those who embody their values.

This discernment helps us forge deeper, more meaningful connections, and steer towards individuals who enhance our lives and support our self-actualization. It underscores that lasting change in ourselves, and our relationships comes not merely through words but through the transformative power of actions.

Recognizing the importance of actions helps build a social circle that truly reflects and supports our values and aspirations. By aligning with people whose actions confirm their integrity, we foster relationships based on trust and mutual respect, essential for lasting bonds.

In leadership and management, the principle teaches us that leaders who lead by example, demonstrating expected behaviors themselves, are far more effective. This approach not only establishes credibility but also fosters an environment of accountability and respect.

In personal settings, recognizing disparities between words and actions protects us from disappointments and informs our decisions about whom to trust. It empowers us to set healthy boundaries with those whose actions do not align with their words, maintaining our well-being and peace of mind.

The focus on actions over words should also influence how we perceive and present ourselves. Ensuring that our actions consistently reflect our values not only strengthens our character but positions us as reliable, principled individuals.
Moreover, embracing a culture of action encourages a more proactive, engaged approach in all life aspects. Whether pursuing personal goals, engaging in community service, or undertaking professional projects, prioritizing actions fosters a productive environment.

Turning Insights into Alerts

As we transition from exploring how actions reveal true character, we now turn our attention to recognizing the warning signs that can signal potential issues in our relationships, as well as the positive indicators that denote healthy connections. This shift from evaluating integrity through actions to actively spotting red flags in interactions, as well as identifying green flags that signify positive qualities, is essential for maintaining healthy, supportive connections.

2.3 Identifying Red Flags (Green Flags)

In the early pages of this book, we introduced a metaphor—a crossroad where every person encountered becomes a pivotal signpost shaping our path of personal growth. This section expands upon that imagery. Picture yourself once more at that crossroad, but this time, you are equipped with the discernment of red flags and green flags. Navigating the intricacies of human relationships demands a sharp awareness of both: red flags, which are warning signs of potential challenges, and green flags, which are indicators of positive qualities. This section will explore eight critical red and green flags that can help you develop keen perception. This enhanced awareness not only nurtures connections that fuel our growth and well-being but also shields us from potential harm, steering us toward deeply-fulfilling relationships. Just like how the Violations poster created by Sydney's softball team fostered accountability and strengthened their sense of community, our ability to identify these flags can similarly enhance our relational landscapes. You're now at a crossroad that has signals.

1. Consistency Between Words and Actions

As we discussed in the previous section, trustworthiness in any relationship is fundamentally dependent on the consistency between words and actions. If there is a frequent discrepancy where promises are not fulfilled or actions contradict verbal commitments, it indicates a misalignment between a person's professed values and their actual behavior. This inconsistency not only undermines trust but also suggests deeper issues with honesty and integrity—key pillars of any healthy relationship. Identifying and addressing these discrepancies early on can prevent misunderstandings and foster a more transparent and reliable connection.

Green Flag: Demonstrates consistency in honoring commitments, follows through on promises, and aligns actions with stated values, building trust and fostering security in relationships.

2. Emotional Manipulation and Gaslighting

Emotional manipulation and gaslighting represent severe threats to relationship health. These tactics involve manipulating another's feelings to gain control and can include undermining a person's perception of reality, leading to confusion and self-doubt. Recognizing these behaviors early is essential for safeguarding one's mental health and setting clear boundaries.

It's important to seek support to counteract the potentially devastating effects of such psychological abuse.

Green Flag: Engages in open, honest, and respectful communication, avoiding manipulative tactics and prioritizing mutual understanding and emotional safety.

3. Jealousy and Possessiveness

Extreme jealousy and possessiveness often surface through unreasonable demands, accusations, or restrictions, reflecting deep-seated insecurity and a desire for control. These behaviors not only infringe on personal freedom but also create a suffocating and toxic environment that impedes emotional growth and well-being. Addressing these issues often requires clear communication about boundaries and, in some cases, professional help to resolve underlying insecurities.

Green Flag: Respects personal boundaries and autonomy, encourages individual growth and freedom, and fosters a supportive and trusting environment.

4. Inability to Take Responsibility

An inability to take responsibility for personal actions is a significant red flag in any relationship. Individuals who habitually shift blame to others or external circumstances often display a lack of maturity and accountability. This trait can undermine relationship dynamics and is frequently associated with disrespect for personal boundaries, contributing to a broader pattern of emotional instability and potential abuse.

Green Flag: Acknowledges mistakes, takes responsibility for actions, and demonstrates a willingness to learn and grow, fostering accountability and mutual respect.

5. Financial Irresponsibility and Dishonesty

Habitual overspending or lying about financial transactions are indicative of a disregard for not only personal financial health but also the stability of the relationship. These behaviors can severely strain partnerships, erode trust, and lead to significant conflicts. Addressing these issues may involve setting financial boundaries, seeking financial counseling, or reevaluating the relationship's viability.

Green Flag: Practices financial transparency, honesty, and responsibility, collaboratively managing finances and respecting mutual financial goals and boundaries.

6. Substance Abuse and Addiction

Substance abuse and addiction introduce significant challenges into relationships, often manifesting as behaviors that prioritize the addiction over the relationship's health. This might include deceit, theft, or emotional manipulation to support the addiction. Recognizing these signs early and seeking professional intervention can be pivotal in managing these behaviors effectively. Support groups and therapy can also play an integral role in recovery and in maintaining the health of the relationship.

Green Flag: Engages in healthy coping mechanisms, seeks professional help when needed, and prioritizes the well-being of self and others over addictive behaviors.

7. Verbal and Emotional Abuse

Making derogatory comments or attempts to undermine someone's self-esteem can have deeply damaging effects on an individual's mental health. These behaviors are designed to belittle or intimidate, creating an environment of fear and dependency. Recognizing and addressing these actions promptly is essential, as they can escalate and become more destructive over time. Support from mental health professionals and trusted individuals is essential for the victim to regain confidence and ensure their safety.

Green Flag: Communicates respectfully, avoids derogatory language or actions, and promotes a positive and uplifting atmosphere in the relationship.

8. Unhealthy Power Dynamics

Unhealthy power dynamics in a relationship, where one party excessively influences decisions or dominates the other, can undermine the mutual respect and equality that are fundamental to any healthy partnership. Such dynamics can manifest as one partner making most decisions without consultation or respecting the other's autonomy. It's important to recognize and rectify these dynamics to restore balance, ensuring that both parties feel valued and respected in the relationship.

Green Flag: Values and respects each other's autonomy, collaborates on decisions, and maintains a balanced and equitable relationship dynamic.

Let's pause and imagine a different scenario—a crossroad devoid of any signals. Picture a bustling intersection, teeming with traffic but lacking any traffic lights to guide or control the flow. The result is predictable: confusion reigns, with vehicles and pedestrians unsure of when to stop or go, leading to potential mishaps and chaos. This visualization serves as a metaphor for navigating relationships without the awareness of red flags and green flags. Without these indicators, we risk entering or staying in situations that may not only hinder our growth but also lead us into conflicts or emotional turmoil. Recognizing and understanding the significance of these signals is akin to having traffic lights at a busy intersection—they provide the guidance needed to move forward safely and confidently in our relationships. Considering each situation within its context and observing behaviors over time, rather than making snap judgments based on a single action, is essential. Mindfully noting both red flags and green flags allows for a balanced perspective in navigating relationships, ensuring that we proceed with both caution and optimism where appropriate.

From Observation to Self-Evaluation

Having explored both red flags, which serve as warning signs in relationships, and green flags, which indicate positive qualities, we now shift our focus inward to reflect on the outcomes of our actions and relationships. This transition from external observation to self-evaluation is essential as we strive for personal growth and self-actualization. In the upcoming section, we will delve into various methods that empower us to assess the quality and impact of our interpersonal connections and personal achievements.

2.4 Evaluating Your "Fruit"

Evaluating our life's outcomes and relationships is essential as we strive for personal growth and self-actualization. This evaluative process demands self-awareness, objective observation, and a commitment to continuous improvement. It helps us understand the trajectory of our personal development and the depth of our interpersonal connections. In this section, we will explore seven key techniques that facilitate this evaluation. These methods will guide us in assessing how well our deeds and behaviors align with our broader life goals and values, and how our relationships contribute to or detract from our overall well-being.

1. The Role of Self-Reflection

Self-reflection is essential for understanding our behaviors and their motivations. Techniques like journaling, meditation, or quiet contemplation enable us to examine our life choices and their impacts critically. This introspection should be balanced with self-compassion, allowing us to identify both strengths and areas for improvement without self-judgment. For example, journaling might reveal that improving your response to stress could significantly enhance both personal and professional relationships. Regular self-reflection deepens our understanding and aligns our actions with our broader life goals and values.

2. Seeking and Utilizing Objective Feedback

Receiving objective feedback from trusted sources such as friends, mentors, or colleagues is invaluable. Keeping an open mind to feedback that challenges your self-perception is essential. For instance, a mentor might highlight a pattern in your decision-making that you hadn't noticed, providing critical insights for your career development. Creating a feedback-rich environment supports continuous personal growth and promotes a culture of openness in your relationships.

3. Incorporating Mindfulness and Regular Assessments

Incorporating daily mindfulness and regular assessments of your progress towards personal goals is essential for maintaining awareness of your actions and their impacts. Mindfulness keeps you present, enhancing your consciousness in daily interactions and allowing you to observe the immediate effects of your behaviors on your relationships and well-being. This continuous monitoring helps you adjust your behaviors to better reflect your core values and aspirations.

4. Evaluating Relationship Health

Continually assessing the health of your relationships is key to ensuring they contribute positively to your well-being. Regular evaluations can help determine if certain interactions are energizing or draining, guiding you on whether to nurture or reconsider these relationships. Healthy relationships should support your growth and fulfillment, and regular assessments help maintain this supportive network.

5. Making Evaluation a Habit

Integrating evaluation techniques into your daily routine turns the assessment of your life's outcomes into a habit. This practice enables informed decision-making and timely adjustments that align with your values and aspirations. By consistently evaluating your actions and their results, you can let go of what no longer serves you and foster growth in beneficial areas.

6. Adapting to Life's Constant Changes

Recognizing that both your life and relationships are dynamic and constantly evolving is essential. What may be beneficial at one stage can become less so as circumstances change, necessitating adaptations in your approach to personal goals and relationships. This flexibility helps you stay aligned with your evolving needs and aspirations.

7. Committing to Regular Evaluation and Adaptation

Committing to regular evaluation and adaptation empowers you to live intentionally and authentically. This commitment ensures that your actions consistently reflect your deepest values, leading to a life that is not only fulfilling but also true to your personal and professional aspirations. By embracing continual self-evaluation and adaptation, you ensure that your life's outcomes are meaningful and deeply rewarding.

Implementing these techniques is not without its challenges. For example, finding time for regular self-reflection or facing uncomfortable truths in feedback can be daunting. Setting aside dedicated time for reflection and viewing feedback as a valuable tool for growth can help overcome these barriers.

Having delved into the techniques for evaluating the "fruit" of our own life and relationships, we now advance our understanding by examining case studies that embody these principles. This next section showcases individuals who exemplify the outcomes of living according to their values and the consequences of failing to do so. Through these narratives, we gain insights into how the abstract concepts discussed previously manifest in tangible actions and their ripple effects on both personal lives and broader societal contexts. These stories not only illustrate the profound impact of our choices but also reinforce the importance of continuous self-evaluation and adaptation in pursuit of a fulfilling and ethically-sound life.

2.5 Case Studies

The Good

Keanu Reeves

Keanu Reeves, celebrated for his roles in blockbuster films such as "The Matrix" and "John Wick," is equally known for his down-to-earth personality and extraordinary generosity. Beyond his acting career, Reeves has made headlines for his numerous acts of kindness, including substantial donations to children's hospitals and cancer research, though he often does so anonymously to avoid personal publicity. Additionally, he is known to have given away much of his earnings from the Matrix series to the special effects and makeup staff, recognizing their contributions to the film's success. His approachable and selfless nature makes him a beloved figure not only in Hollywood but also by the general public, setting an example of humility and philanthropy in an industry often criticized for its superficiality.

David Green

As the founder of Hobby Lobby, David Green has built his business on principles rooted in his Christian faith, which significantly influences the company's operations, including closing stores on Sundays and fighting legal battles to uphold his religious beliefs against government mandates. Under his leadership, Hobby Lobby has grown to over 900 stores in the U.S., and he commits a substantial portion of the company's profits to philanthropy, particularly Christian organizations. His stance on integrating faith with business operations has sparked national conversations about the role of religion in business and the rights of business owners to operate their companies in line with their spiritual convictions.

Malala Yousafzai

Malala Yousafzai, a Pakistani activist for female education, became the youngest-ever Nobel Prize laureate in recognition of her struggles against the suppression of children and young people and for the right of all children to education. Surviving a Taliban assassination attempt at just 15 years old, she co-founded the Malala Fund to bring attention to the educational deficits worldwide. Malala's advocacy has had a global impact, pushing education issues to the forefront of social and political agendas in many countries and inspiring countless other young women to pursue education and demand their rights.

Tim Tebow

Known for his career in professional football and baseball, Tim Tebow is also prominent for his devout Christian faith, which he has integrated into his public persona and philanthropic efforts. Through the Tim Tebow Foundation, founded in 2010, he has provided support for children with life-threatening illnesses and launched numerous initiatives to help the underprivileged, both domestically and internationally. His foundation's work includes building playrooms in hospitals, supporting adoption, and hosting a worldwide prom event for special needs children called "Night to Shine."

Thomas Sowell

Thomas Sowell is an American economist, social theorist, and senior fellow at Stanford University's Hoover Institution. Sowell has written extensively on economic policy, racial relations, and the history of ideas. Renowned for his conservative viewpoints and incisive critiques of liberal policies, Sowell's work emphasizes empirical evidence and clear-eyed analysis over political correctness. His books and columns--which address a wide range of topics from economic theory to social policy and cultural issues--have influenced public thought and policy debates significantly.

Each of the individuals above embodies the principle of living out one's values in a public and impactful way, influencing their respective fields and broader societal norms through their actions and commitments.

The Bad and The Ugly

Harvey Weinstein

Harvey Weinstein was a dominant force in Hollywood as the co-founder of Miramax and The Weinstein Company, known for producing iconic films like “Pulp Fiction,” “Shakespeare in Love,” and “The King's Speech.” However, in October of 2017, Weinstein's illustrious career collapsed under the weight of numerous allegations of sexual harassment and assault published by The New York Times and The New Yorker, with some accusations dating back decades. This led to his dismissal from his company and being ostracized by various film academies. His actions catalyzed the #MeToo movement, leading to global discussions on sexual misconduct in the workplace and beyond. In February of 2020, Weinstein was convicted of rape and sexual assault, receiving a 23-year prison sentence, marking a significant moment in addressing sexual misconduct across industries.

Jussie Smollett

Jussie Smollett, best known for his role in the television series “Empire,” became embroiled in controversy in January of 2019 when he reported being the victim of a racist and homophobic attack. An investigation by the Chicago Police Department later revealed that Smollett had orchestrated the attack himself, purportedly to advance his career and increase his salary. This led to charges against him for filing a false police report and disorderly conduct. The incident sparked a widespread public debate on the serious implications of fabricating hate crimes, highlighting the potential harm to the credibility of actual victims.

Brian Williams

Brian Williams, once a respected anchor on NBC Nightly News, faced a career-defining scandal in 2015 when he admitted to embellishing an account of his experiences during the Iraq War, particularly a helicopter incident in 2003. His admission led to a six-month suspension without pay and significantly damaged his credibility. Williams was subsequently reassigned to a lesser role at MSNBC--NBC's sister network. His downfall is frequently referenced in discussions about the critical need for integrity in journalism.

Lance Armstrong

Lance Armstrong, celebrated for winning the Tour de France seven times and overcoming testicular cancer, saw his legacy unravel in 2012 following a report by the US Anti-Doping Agency that detailed his involvement in a comprehensive doping program. Armstrong was stripped of his Tour de France titles and banned for life from professional cycling. He later admitted to doping in a 2013 interview with Oprah Winfrey. The scandal not only tarnished his reputation but also had a lasting impact on the cycling community and his cancer support charity, Livestrong.

Michael Avenatti

Michael Avenatti, an attorney known for representing Stormy Daniels in her lawsuits against Donald Trump, was arrested in 2019 for attempting to extort up to $25 million from Nike. Avenatti threatened to release damaging information about the company unless they agreed to hire him for an internal investigation. In 2020, he was convicted of extortion and sentenced to 2.5 years in prison, facing additional charges of embezzlement and fraud. Avenatti's case has become a cautionary tale about the dangers of power abuse and misconduct in the legal profession, severely damaging his reputation and highlighting ethical concerns in legal practices.

Another “Dinner Test”

Like the Dinner Test in Chapter 1, let's envision stepping into the same bustling restaurant with someone significant to you. As you survey the scene, two distinct tables vie for your attention.

At the Table of Integrity, you'll find individuals revered for their integrity and positive contributions: Keanu Reeves, celebrated for his extraordinary generosity; David Green, whose business integrates ethical practices with deep personal faith; Malala Yousafzai, an unwavering advocate for education; Tim Tebow, committed to supporting those in need; and Thomas Sowell, renowned for his impactful intellectual insights. This table embodies integrity, compassion, and a profound societal influence.

Conversely, the second table—the Table of Controversy--hosts a group embodying controversy: Harvey Weinstein, Jussie Smollett, Brian Williams, Lance Armstrong, and Michael Avenatti. Here, the complexities of ethical lapses and personal failures are evident.

Now, picture two additional tables behind each initial table, each with ten more individuals:

Table of Integrity Additions:

- Abigail Johnson: Known for ethical leadership in the financial industry.
- Albert Pujols: Renowned for his philanthropic efforts and community support.
- Brian Chesky: Focused on innovation and creating positive experiences for travelers.
- Emma Stone: Advocates for various charitable causes and social justice initiatives.
- Eric Yuan: Pioneers advancements in technology with integrity and transparency.
- Jensen Huang: Demonstrates ethical business practices in the tech sector.
- Mary Barra: Leads with integrity and accountability in the automotive industry.

- Matthew McConaughey: Known for his charitable work and inspirational speeches.
- Reed Hastings: Fosters a culture of innovation and integrity in the entertainment industry.
- Susan Wojcicki: Defied expectations by excelling as a top executive and mother of five.

Table of Controversy Additions:

- Adam Neumann: Involved in controversial business practices and leadership decisions at WeWork.
- Andrew Mason: Faced scrutiny for management decisions during his tenure at Groupon.
- Bill Cosby: Controversial figure due to allegations of sexual assault.
- Dara Khosrowshahi: Dealt with controversies and criticisms during his leadership at Uber.
- David Wildstein: Known for involvement in the Bridgegate scandal in New Jersey.
- Dennis Muilenburg: Criticized for Boeing's handling of the 737 MAX crisis.
- Ellen DeGeneres: Faced controversy and workplace culture issues on her talk show.
- Marissa Mayer: Criticized for management decisions and handling of Yahoo's challenges.

- Martin Winterkorn: Involved in the Volkswagen emissions scandal during his tenure as CEO.
- R. Kelly: Controversial figure due to allegations of sexual abuse and misconduct.

Reflecting on Chapter 1, consider what values and potential outcomes sway your decision regarding which table you'd sit at. This exercise transcends mere seating choices. It prompts deep reflection on the profound impact our company has on personal and professional lives. Returning to this scenario encourages an assessment, not just of individuals, but of the principles and values they embody, shaping our choices and reflections on the circles we keep.

2.6 Recognizing the Fruit: Five Key Takeaways

1. Remember that Actions Speak Louder Than Words

   The reliability of a person's character is most accurately judged by their actions rather than their promises or statements. Continuous observation of someone's actions across different situations is essential for understanding their true intentions and reliability. This approach helps to discern sincerity from pretense, offering a clearer picture of who they really are.

2. Embrace Vulnerability and Authenticity

   Creating a supportive atmosphere that encourages vulnerability and authenticity allows for deeper and more meaningful relationships. Cultivate an environment where openness and emotional honesty are valued, enabling you and those around you to express your true selves without fear of judgment. This foundation of trust is essential for lasting, supportive relationships that foster mutual growth.

3. Prioritize Integrity and Accountability

Integrity and accountability are cornerstones of trustworthy relationships. Seek out and cherish associations with individuals who consistently demonstrate ethical behavior and are willing to own their actions and decisions. Steer clear of those who habitually dodge responsibility or manipulate truths, as these behaviors can undermine mutual trust and respect.

4. Cultivate Emotional Intelligence and Maturity

Emotional intelligence and maturity are key traits that enhance the quality of interactions and relationships. Prioritize connections with individuals who demonstrate these qualities, particularly the ability to navigate complex emotions and handle conflict with poise. Such individuals tend to be more understanding, making them invaluable companions in both personal and professional settings.

5. Commit to Self-Reflection and Growth

Commit to lifelong self-reflection and personal growth so that your actions consistently mirror your values and aspirations. Regular self-assessment, along with an openness to receiving constructive feedback, facilitates continual improvement and adaptation. This practice not only bolsters personal integrity but also helps maintain alignment between your relationships and your evolving values and goals.

2.7 Recognizing the Fruit: Ten Key Questions

1. Identify the top three values you seek in others. How well do the people closest to you embody these values?
2. Can you recall a time when someone's actions contradicted their words? What did this reveal about their true character?
3. What red flags have you overlooked in relationships, and what were the consequences of ignoring them?
4. Which case study discussed was most impactful for you in understanding character and relationship dynamics? Why?
5. How have your criteria for assessing character changed after reading this section?
6. What steps will you take to better discern actions over words in your relationships?
7. Think of a relationship where you overlooked warning signs. What would you do differently now?
8. How do you plan to apply the techniques for evaluating relationship outcomes in the future?
9. What changes will you make in assessing new and existing relationships based on the insights from this section?

10. Given the scenario presented in “Another Dinner Test,” which table would you choose to sit at? Describe your reasons for your choice and how it aligns with your core values and personal goals.

Cultivating Growth: From Recognition to Pruning

As we conclude our examination of "Recognizing the Fruit," we now transition to the next significant phase in our personal development. Chapter 3, "Pruning for Growth," shifts our focus from recognition to action. We will explore the necessity of letting go of unproductive or toxic relationships and practices. This natural progression from understanding to action emphasizes the importance of not only identifying what does not serve us but also taking decisive steps to remove these obstacles. By learning how to effectively prune our lives of the negative influences and habits we've identified, we pave the way for new growth, enhanced well-being, and improved relationships that truly reflect and support our highest aspirations.

Chapter 3. Pruning for Growth

A.D. Posey

“"Everyone grows old, but not everyone grows up.”[7]

[7] The quote "Everyone grows old, but not everyone grows up" by A.D. Posey captures a significant insight about maturity. It suggests that while aging is an inevitable, natural process, growing up in terms of emotional and psychological maturity requires more intentional effort and self-reflection. Posey's words emphasize the distinction between merely aging physically and evolving maturely through life's experiences, highlighting that personal growth is not automatically guaranteed as one ages.

The Denny's Dilemma Part 3: "Policy of Truth"

After my plea, the manager expressed surprise at the situation, noting that most dine-and-dashes typically result in lost revenue. He mentioned something that struck me deeply: "If Sue kept a better eye on your friends, you wouldn't have to bail them out." While I rectified the situation, it felt like I had traded one burden for another.

But our server wasn't just a faceless employee. How much trouble did she face because of our actions? She's a waitress at Denny's, working hard at 2:00 AM on a Saturday, likely out of necessity rather than choice. What if she loses her job? Is she a single mother? I was an asshole. I played asshole games, so I got asshole prizes.

3.1 Ending Unproductive/Toxic Relationships

Understanding the need to let go of unproductive and toxic relationships is critical for personal growth and well-being. These relationships, whether stagnant or actively harmful, sap our resources and hinder our development. They range from unproductive connections that offer no mutual support or inspiration, merely occupying space in our lives, to toxic ones that undermine our well-being through manipulation, criticism, and emotional abuse. Recognizing and acting to end these relationships is essential for freeing up emotional and physical space for more fulfilling connections.

Unproductive relationships merely exist without adding value, while toxic relationships actively damage our well-being, leaving us diminished and stressed. Acknowledging the need to move on involves an honest assessment of each relationship's impact on our lives and recognizing their detrimental effects. The cost of maintaining these relationships is high—not only do they consume time and energy, but the stress and negativity they bring can also infiltrate other areas of our lives, affecting our mental health, productivity, and overall happiness.

Letting go is a reaffirmation of our self-worth and a declaration of our right to healthier relationships. It requires courage, self-awareness, and a firm commitment to our well-being. This process may involve tough conversations, setting boundaries, or even ending relationships. Support from friends, family, or professionals is invaluable during this time, offering needed perspective and emotional support.

As we clear out negative influences, it's essential to nurture the relationships that positively impact our lives—those that offer mutual respect, trust, and encouragement to grow. The act of letting go is not just about eliminating the negative but also about making room for new, positive experiences. This dynamic, ongoing process of reassessment and realignment evolves as our needs and circumstances change.

By embracing this process of letting go, we commit to a life where our relationships reflect our values and aspirations, enhancing our path toward fulfillment and success. Letting go is not a sign of failure but a proactive step towards a healthier existence.

This transformative process includes seven key principals:

1. Emotional Detoxification

Liberating ourselves from toxic emotions and patterns is essential for achieving mental and emotional clarity and resilience. Emotional detoxification involves identifying and letting go of negative emotions such as anger, resentment, or fear, which often stem from past experiences or unhealthy relationships. This process enables us to approach life and new relationships with a more positive, clear perspective, and supports our overall mental health, allowing us to respond to new challenges with greater composure and effectiveness.

2. Boundaries and Self-Care

Setting clear boundaries is essential for maintaining not only healthy relationships but also our personal well-being. Boundaries help define what we are comfortable with and how we expect to be treated by others. Boundaries are essential for preserving our self-esteem and energy levels. Establishing limits ensures that we engage in self-care by not allowing others to overstep and *take* more from us than we are willing or able to *give*. This practice is fundamental in fostering self-respect and ensuring that our relationships contribute positively to our lives.

3. Authentic Connections

Fostering genuine relationships that are built on mutual respect and trust is key to enhancing our sense of belonging and personal growth. Authentic connections involve open communication, vulnerability, and a deep understanding of each other's needs and desires. These relationships enrich our lives, providing emotional support and motivation to pursue our goals. They also create a safe space for personal discovery and the mutual exchange of ideas that propel personal development.

4. Lifestyle Alignment

Assessing how relationships align with our lifestyle and goals is essential for maintaining focus and direction in life. This alignment involves ensuring that the people we choose to spend time with not only understand but also support our life's ambitions and the lifestyle choices we make. When our relationships are congruent with our goals, they naturally propel us forward, providing encouragement and making it easier to achieve our objectives.

5. Continuous Evaluation

Regular reassessment of our relationships is necessary to ensure they remain healthy and fulfilling. Continuous evaluation helps us recognize when a relationship may no longer be beneficial or when it may be causing more harm than good. This ongoing process allows us to make informed decisions about which relationships we should nurture and which we might need to reconsider or end.

6. Self-Reflection and Growth

Engaging in self-reflection is pivotal in enhancing our self-awareness, which in turn helps us better understand our relationship dynamics and personal habits. Through self-reflection, we can identify areas where we may need improvement, whether in communication, empathy, or conflict resolution. This introspection supports our personal development by allowing us to address our weaknesses, capitalize on our strengths, and evolve into more compassionate and understanding individuals.

7. Gratitude and Letting Go

Embracing the lessons from past relationships and letting go of them with gratitude is an important step in moving forward and making room for new growth and connections. Recognizing the value and lessons each relationship has provided, regardless of its outcome, enables us to release emotional baggage and bitterness. This act of gratitude not only fosters a positive mindset but also clears the path for new relationships that can bring fresh perspectives and opportunities into our lives.

Integrating these seven principles into our lives creates a holistic framework for personal transformation and healthy relationship management. This not only uplifts us but it also enhances our social interactions, creating a supportive and thriving environment for everyone involved.

The Growth Continuum

As we acknowledge the significance of releasing unproductive and toxic relationships, we naturally segue into a more comprehensive approach to personal development. This approach, known as "pruning," extends beyond just distancing ourselves from negative influences; it encompasses refining all aspects of our lives to foster growth and enhance well-being. Pruning involves not only removing obstacles to our progress but also actively cultivating habits, mindsets, and environments that support our overall success and fulfillment. As we talk more about the concept of pruning in the next section, we will explore how this deliberate process is fundamental in shaping a life that is not only free from hindrances, but also rich with opportunities for personal and professional development.

3.2 The Concept of Pruning

Pruning, in the context of personal growth, involves carefully assessing and refining various aspects of our lives to enhance our development and achieve our full potential. This process is essential. It helps us remove elements that hinder progress and nurture those that contribute positively to our well-being and success. In this section, we will explore six key concepts of pruning: refining our habits, reevaluating our beliefs and thought patterns, enhancing relationships, optimizing our physical environment, aligning our lifestyle choices, and embracing continuous assessment and adjustment. As you read each of these concepts, notice how they play an integral role in fostering an environment that supports our overall growth.

1. Refining Habits

Positive habits, such as regular exercise and continuous learning, drive personal growth by improving our health and broadening our skills. In contrast, negative habits like procrastination and excessive social media consumption can sap our energy and distract from our goals. Effective pruning requires us to honestly evaluate our routines and replace detrimental habits with constructive ones. This change demands discipline, self-awareness, and a steadfast commitment to growth.

2. Transforming Beliefs and Thought Patterns

Limiting beliefs can create mental barriers that cap our potential, while negative thought patterns can skew our perceptions and reactions to life's challenges. By adopting a growth mindset, we can replace these limiting beliefs with empowering ones, enhancing our resilience and adaptability. This mental shift is essential for fostering a positive, solution-oriented approach that turns challenges into opportunities for growth.

3. Elevating Relationships

Relationships profoundly influence our personal and professional development. Positive connections stimulate growth, whereas toxic relationships can drain our energy and impede our progress. Pruning in this domain may involve difficult decisions, such as setting boundaries or ending detrimental relationships, which--although challenging--affirm our self-worth and commitment to personal well-being.

4. Broadening Network Quality

Beyond personal relationships, our professional and community interactions also play a significant role in our development. Actively cultivating relationships that align with our goals and values encourages mutual growth and opens opportunities for collaboration and achievement. This selective engagement in our broader networks ensures that our social and professional interactions support our overall aspirations.

5. Creating Space for New Opportunities

Pruning is not merely about cutting away the negative; it's about making room for new growth. This ongoing process requires us to continually evaluate and adjust our habits, beliefs, and relationships to ensure they align with our evolving goals and circumstances.

6. Lifestyle and Environment Adjustments

Extending the pruning process to our physical surroundings and lifestyle choices can further enhance our clarity and focus. An organized, clutter-free environment and intentional lifestyle choices in diet, sleep, and recreation can significantly boost our mental and physical health.

Progressing from Pruning to Closure

As we refine our habits and realign our lifestyles through pruning, it becomes evident that relationships themselves sometimes require reassessment. The principles of pruning that we apply to our habits and beliefs are equally essential when considering our personal and professional relationships. This process is not just about removing what hinders us but also about fostering relationships that support our growth. Next, we will talk about practical strategies for gracefully ending relationships that no longer serve us. This step is essential because it allows us to dedicate our energy and resources to connections that are nurturing and align with our path toward personal fulfillment and success. By understanding how to end these relationships with compassion and respect, our social environment can continue to support our development and well-being.

3.3 How to End Relationships That No Longer Serve You

Ending relationships that no longer contribute to your growth is a crucial aspect of personal development and emotional well-being. This intricate process demands a delicate balance of compassion, assertiveness, and self-respect, with clear communication and kindness as its foundation. This section presents seven steps to effectively terminate such relationships, ensuring that you navigate the process with sensitivity while safeguarding your well-being.

1. Initiate Closure

Start with a thorough introspection of the relationship's dynamics to pinpoint the aspects that hinder your personal growth. This phase is critical as it helps you understand what specifically needs to change. Reflect deeply on patterns of interaction that have led to stagnation or distress. Evaluate how these patterns conflict with your personal values and goals and prepare to articulate these conflicts clearly when you communicate your decision.

2. Understand Emotions

Allow yourself to fully experience and process your emotions related to the relationship. Whether it's sadness, disappointment, or even relief, understanding these feelings is foundational for communicating effectively and honestly. This emotional clarity aids in expressing your decision with authenticity and can prevent future regrets.

3. Communicate Decisively

When it's time to convey your decision, do so with unequivocal clarity to avoid prolonging distress or confusion. Be direct yet compassionate, using "I" statements to take ownership of your feelings and to minimize defensiveness. For example: "I've realized that this relationship is no longer beneficial to my personal growth. It's important for me to move on."

4. Maintain Open Dialogue

Engage in a respectful dialogue where both parties can share their views. Too often as a society, we tend to listen to respond rather than listen to hear. It's important to listen actively, but also to reaffirm your boundaries to ensure that the conversation remains constructive. This dialogue can help both parties understand each other's perspectives and facilitate a more amicable separation.

5. Prioritize Self-Care

Invest in self-care practices that maintain or improve your emotional and physical well-being during this transitional period. Activities like mindfulness meditation, physical exercise, and engaging in hobbies can significantly aid your emotional resilience. This is a great time to "hang out" with yourself, so to speak. Additionally, seek support from friends, family, or a professional counselor to provide perspective and coping strategies.

6. Navigate Post-Relationship Dynamics

If the relationship is deeply integrated into your social or professional life, plan a gradual disengagement. This strategy minimizes disruption and emotional upheaval, allowing for a smoother adjustment to the new status quo. Communicate your intentions clearly to mutual friends or colleagues to avoid misunderstandings and to maintain support networks. In simpler terms, don't "bite off" more than you can chew.

7. Embrace Forgiveness and Compassion

Approach the conclusion of the relationship with forgiveness and compassion, recognizing that both parties have likely contributed to the situation in some way. Embracing forgiveness can dramatically reduce your emotional burden and aid in healing.

Celebrate the growth you've experienced as a result of this relationship and acknowledge the positive aspects that existed.

From Ending to Enhancing Relationships

Transitioning from gracefully ending relationships to cultivating fruitful ones is a natural progression in personal growth. After making the difficult but necessary decision to close chapters that no longer align with our evolving goals and aspirations, it becomes equally important to focus on nurturing relationships that contribute positively to our development. As we release the old, we pave the way to embrace the new. We make room for relationships that offer mutual growth, respect, and alignment with our personal and professional objectives. Next, we'll talk about how we can actively cultivate and maintain such growth-promoting relationships, ensuring that our social environment remains vibrant, supportive, and aligned with our path to personal fulfillment.

3.4 How to Sustain Growth-Focused Relationships

In the dynamic process of personal development, it becomes imperative to continually assess the influence of our interpersonal relationships. As our goals and values evolve, so too must our social circle. Relationships that once provided support and nurtured our growth may no longer align with our current aspirations, necessitating careful reconsideration. This section delves into the multifaceted process of recognizing when relationships cease to contribute positively to our development through ten essential steps. These ten steps, from recognizing the need for change, to embracing new opportunities for transformation, are essential for safeguarding our emotional well-being and ensuring our social environment fosters our overall success and fulfillment. While this framework covers a comprehensive pathway, it is important to remember that the process of managing relationships can involve additional nuances and personal adaptations.

1. Recognize the Need for Change

As we progress on our personal development journey, we may find that certain relationships no longer align with our evolving values, goals, or well-being. Relationships that were once supportive can transform into obstacles that hinder our personal growth. It's essential to be vigilant and recognize when a relationship shifts from beneficial to detrimental. This awareness is fundamental as it prompts a proactive approach to managing your social circle, which is the first step toward fostering an environment conducive to your personal development.

2. Assess Your Relationships

Evaluating your relationships involves deep introspection and honesty. Reflect on the dynamics of each of your relationships by asking yourself these key questions: What has changed? How does this relationship currently affect your emotional and mental state? Do these interactions uplift you or bring you down? Such thorough reflection will help you understand the negative impacts more comprehensively and will lay a strong foundation for any necessary decisions. This stage is about gathering insight that will inform your actions, ensuring they are based on a clear understanding of the impact each relationship has on your life.

3. Decide to Disconnect

Choosing to distance yourself from a relationship that no longer contributes positively to your life is a significant and often difficult decision that requires courage and integrity. Approach this decision with clarity and purpose, ensuring that your actions are not impulsive but rather the result of careful consideration. When communicating your decision, prioritize transparency and kindness to minimize hurt feelings and conflict. Employ "I" statements to express your feelings and clarify your needs, making it clear that the decision is about your personal growth and not a judgment of the other person.

4. Communicate Your Decision

When the time comes to articulate your decision, do so with directness, honesty, and compassion. Clear communication is critical to prevent misunderstandings and clarify your intentions. It is important to be firm and decisive to eliminate any ambiguity about your stance. This step involves balancing assertiveness with empathy, acknowledging the past value of the relationship while being clear about why it can no longer continue in the same form.

5. Set Boundaries

Once you have decided to change the nature of a relationship, establishing and maintaining clear boundaries is essential. Define what is acceptable behavior and the extent of future interactions, which might range from limited contact to ending the relationship entirely. Effective boundaries ensure that both parties understand the new dynamics, which helps prevent potential conflicts and discomfort moving forward.

6. Manage the Transition

If the relationship is deeply integrated into your personal or professional life, a gradual disengagement may be necessary. This strategy helps manage the emotional and practical complexities of detaching from someone integral to your daily routines. Gradually reducing interactions can ease the transition for both parties, minimizing disruption and emotional turmoil.

7. Prioritize Self-Care

Throughout this transition, prioritize your emotional and psychological health. Surround yourself with supportive friends and family and engage in activities that nurture your spirit and contribute to your well-being, such as meditation, exercise, or creative pursuits. These practices not only provide therapeutic benefits but also help you remain centered and focused on your growth.

8. Embrace Forgiveness

As you conclude any relationship, approach the process with forgiveness and understanding. Recognize that holding onto grudges or bitterness burdens you with negative emotional baggage. Forgiving is not just about the other person—it's about freeing yourself and moving forward unencumbered by past resentments.

9. Reflect and Learn

After a relationship ends, take time to reflect on the experience. Consider the lessons learned and how these insights can shape your future relationships. This reflection is invaluable as it prepares you to establish more meaningful and supportive connections that better align with your evolving life path.

10. Transform and Grow

View the end of each relationship as an opportunity for personal growth and renewal. Every conclusion brings with it the promise of new beginnings—new connections that will better align with your path and values. Embrace these changes as essential components of your personal development journey, recognizing that each step, even those that involve endings, is a steppingstone to a more fulfilled life.

Transitioning from the principles of relationship management to the practical, real-world consequences of these relationships, we segue into a nuanced examination of case studies that highlight the dramatic effects of the company we keep. After understanding how to cultivate and maintain beneficial relationships, it's enlightening to see these principles in action through the lives of individuals who have navigated both success and adversity. In the forthcoming section, we delve into case studies of Shaquille O'Neal and MC Hammer, whose career trajectories offer profound lessons on the impact of strategic relationship choices and financial decisions. These narratives provide tangible insights into the significant consequences of our social and professional interactions, reinforcing the theories discussed and emphasizing the practical outcomes of wise versus unwise relational investments.

3.5 Case Studies

In the realm of personal development, particularly when discussing the necessity of "pruning" for growth, the stories of Shaquille O'Neal and MC Hammer provide contrasting examples of financial and personal management. This closing section explores how their differing approaches to managing relationships and finances led to distinctly different outcomes in their careers and personal lives, demonstrating the critical importance of judiciously managing one's social and professional circles.

Shaquille O'Neal

Shaquille O'Neal, celebrated as one of basketball's greats, has also made his mark as a shrewd businessman and charismatic media personality. His successful transition from NBA stardom to business mogul showcases a strategic approach to life after sports, marked by a diverse investment portfolio including real estate, brand endorsements, and stakes in ventures from fast-food chains to technology startups.

What sets Shaq apart is his judicious selection of partnerships and endorsement deals. He aligns with brands that resonate with his values and enhance his personal brand, characterized by a blend of affability and savvy business instincts. This selectiveness has not only helped him maintain financial stability but also build a reputation as a reliable, insightful investor.

Shaq's investment philosophy emphasizes understanding market dynamics and recognizing long-term value over immediate gains. His adaptability in navigating post-NBA career opportunities across sports, business, and entertainment, driven by his innate charisma and impeccable timing, demonstrates his market foresight. He carefully selects opportunities that align with his personal and professional goals, demonstrating how sustainable success can be achieved by adhering to one's core values.

His approach extends beyond business to his community involvement and philanthropy, reflecting his commitment to making a social impact. Whether promoting products or engaging in community efforts, Shaq's genuine demeanor and relatability have made him an effective communicator and marketer, garnering respect from peers and fans alike.

Moreover, Shaq advocates for financial literacy, particularly among athletes and young people, underscoring the importance of smart financial planning to manage the transient nature of fame and wealth. The diversity of his investments, including sports teams, esports, and tech startups, highlights his knack for identifying and adapting to emerging trends.

In essence, Shaquille O'Neal's transition from the basketball court to the boardroom provides a blueprint for athletes and entrepreneurs alike, emphasizing strategic planning, personal branding, and the discerning pursuit of opportunities. His story is not just a tale of personal achievement, but also a guide on leveraging one's platform responsibly and effectively, ensuring sustained success and fulfillment.

MC Hammer

MC Hammer, born Stanley Burrell, is often remembered for his meteoric rise to fame and subsequent financial decline. His hit, "U Can't Touch This," epitomized late 1980's pop culture, but his lavish lifestyle and poor financial management eventually led to bankruptcy. Hammer's story serves as a cautionary tale highlighting the dangers of financial mismanagement and overextension.

At the height of his career, Hammer was known for his extravagant spending, including maintaining an entourage of over 200 people. While this showcased his success, it drastically drained his financial resources. The substantial costs associated with supporting such a large entourage, combined with impulsive and poorly researched business ventures, contributed to his financial downfall, culminating in a reported $13 million in debts.

The impact of Hammer's financial mismanagement was profound, affecting both his career and personal life. As his financial stability eroded, so did his ability to sustain his music career and fund new projects. The stress of financial recovery and the public nature of his bankruptcy took a significant personal toll, emphasizing the importance of prudent financial planning and strategic relationship management.

Hammer's experience illustrates the risks associated with excessive spending and the pitfalls of inadequate financial oversight. His situation serves as a lesson for celebrities and public figures on the importance of aligning expenditures with sustainable income, making informed investments, and maintaining a manageable circle of dependents.

Since his bankruptcy, Hammer has reinvented himself, taking on roles such as a tech investor and mentor, to artists and entrepreneurs. This adaptability showcases his resilience and a deeper understanding of the need for diversification and strategic planning in professional endeavors.

MC Hammer's narrative provides insights into the volatility of fame and the critical need for financial literacy and strategic decision-making. His story serves as a stark reminder of the complexities of financial health in the entertainment industry and the broader lesson that success requires a balance of passion, prudence, and planning to sustain it over the long term.

The careers of Shaquille O'Neal and MC Hammer provide striking lessons in the importance of strategic decision-making for personal and professional sustainability. While Shaq has adeptly transitioned from NBA stardom to a successful business magnate with a diversified portfolio, MC Hammer's trajectory serves as a cautionary tale of the consequences of poor financial management and excessive spending. Here we explore four key differences between their approaches: strategic relationships, financial prudence, sustainable growth, and pruning for longevity. Each of these collectively highlight the essential roles of careful relationship management and financial strategy in achieving lasting success.

1. Strategic Relationships

Shaq's ability to forge strategic partnerships has been a cornerstone of his wealth maintenance and growth. He carefully selected relationships that aligned with his long-term goals and supported his transition from basketball to a business career. His partnerships range from major brand endorsements to significant investments in various businesses, reflecting a keen understanding of the value of aligning with the right people and brands. This contrasts sharply with Hammer's approach, who maintained an extensive and costly entourage. His entourage, while large, failed to provide reciprocal benefits, eventually becoming a substantial financial drain that did not contribute to his career or business aspirations.

2. Financial Prudence

Shaq is a paragon of financial prudence, with his investment strategy focusing on ventures that offer growth and security, such as real estate and stock investments in various successful companies. He approaches spending with a mindset geared toward value and long-term returns, which has allowed him to build and maintain a significant fortune. Conversely, Hammer's financial management was characterized by lavish spending on luxuries and maintaining a large entourage without clear financial benefits. His lack of foresight in managing expenditures led to a well-publicized financial collapse, highlighting the critical importance of evaluating each expenditure's long-term value.

3. Sustainable Growth

Post-NBA, Shaq has demonstrated remarkable adaptability, transitioning into roles that extend beyond the sports world into broadcasting, business, and entertainment, thus keeping him relevant and financially robust. He has continuously evolved his brand and business interests to align with changing market dynamics and personal growth objectives. On the other hand, Hammer struggled to adapt his career and financial strategies to the evolving entertainment landscape. His failure to diversify his career focus and adapt to new opportunities severely impacted his financial sustainability and led to a decline in both his career and personal fortune.

4. Pruning for Longevity

Effective pruning of unproductive financial habits and harmful relationships has been essential for Shaq's long-term success. He has demonstrated the ability to cut off ventures or partnerships that no longer serve his broader strategic goals, ensuring his portfolio remains robust and his social connections supportive. This strategic pruning has helped him maintain stability and relevance in various sectors. In contrast, Hammer's reluctance to downsize his entourage or curb his extravagant lifestyle even amid financial difficulties exemplifies a lack of effective pruning. This eventually contributed to his financial downfall, demonstrating that long-term success often requires tough decisions about cutting losses and moving on from relationships that do not contribute to personal or professional growth.

These contrasting narratives of Shaquille O'Neal and MC Hammer vividly demonstrate the impact of personal and financial associations on growth and success. The practice of strategic pruning, essential for sustaining success, involves being selective and thoughtful in relationship and financial decisions. By learning from Shaq's strategic approach and Hammer's missteps, individuals can better navigate their careers and personal growth, ensuring long-term success and fulfillment. These stories not only underscore the importance of wise decision-making but also remind us that sustainable success requires both strategic relationships and financial prudence.

3.6 Pruning for Growth: Five Key Takeaways

1. Letting Go Is an Act of Self-Respect

   Recognizing and ending unproductive or toxic relationships is a courageous act that clears the way for more nurturing connections that better align with your values and support your growth. This step, while often difficult, is a profound demonstration of self-respect and commitment to your personal well-being.

2. Embrace the Pruning Process

   Intentionally eliminate habits, beliefs, or relationships that hinder your progress. Approach this process with compassion and self-awareness, maintaining a firm commitment to your highest good. Pruning isn't merely about cutting away but also about making room for new growth and opportunities that can lead to a more fulfilled and productive life.

3. Graceful Endings Matter

   When ending relationships, it's essential to communicate with honesty and kindness. Set clear boundaries and prioritize self-care to ensure you move forward with grace and resilience. Embracing forgiveness, both for yourself and others, is essential as it frees you from lingering negativity and allows you to embrace the future with optimism.

4. Cultivate Growth-Promoting Relationships

Actively seek and nurture relationships characterized by mutual respect, trust, vulnerability, and a shared commitment to growth. These relationships are the cornerstone of personal and professional development, offering support, inspiration, and new opportunities. It is important to ensure that your connections not only encourage and challenge you but also provide a safe space for personal development.

5. Relationships Shape Your Path

The relationships you maintain have a profound impact on your personal growth and success. By intentionally curating your inner circle, you create an environment that propels you toward realizing your full potential. This involves more than just seeking out positive influences; it also requires mindfulness about how your relationships affect your ambitions and actions.

3.7 Pruning for Growth: Ten Key Questions

1. Have you identified any relationships in your life that are unproductive or toxic? What makes these relationships harmful to your personal growth?
2. How do you understand the concept of pruning in the context of personal relationships? Can you recall a time when removing a certain element (a habit, relationship, or belief) led to healthier personal development?
3. What strategies have you considered or used to end relationships that were no longer beneficial? How did you feel during and after the process?
4. What are the key characteristics of relationships that have promoted your growth? How do you actively cultivate these kinds of relationships?
5. Which case study from this section resonated with you the most, and why? How does it apply to your current situation?
6. What is the most challenging aspect of letting go of unproductive relationships for you, and how do you plan to address this challenge?
7. How has your perspective on the necessity of pruning changed after reading this section?

8. What actionable steps can you take to regularly assess the health of your relationships?
9. Reflect on a relationship you have successfully rejuvenated by addressing issues or setting new boundaries. What lessons did you learn?
10. Moving forward, how will you apply the lessons from this section to better manage or end relationships that do not align with your personal growth goals?

The Denny's Dilemma Part 4: "Close to Me"

A particular phrase from the manager lingered in my mind. Essentially, he shrugged and said, "chalk it up as a loss." That simple remark carried a profound message—not just about the financial loss of $100 but also a personal one. I found myself ready to chalk up my "friends" from the Denny's Dilemma as a loss as well. And that is precisely what happened; I never spoke to them again.

Fast forward to today. Through social media, I've pieced together the lives of the Denny's cast: Heather, a resilient divorced mother of two, still strikingly attractive, working for a plastic surgeon; Beth, happily married for over 25 years, embracing her roles as mother, wife, and grandmother; Mike, a mystery figure, a shadow in the digital realm, later revealed to be on probation related to computers; and then there's James, elusive yet a poignant reminder of the connections I needed to let go of.

As for me? Now, 36 years later, I'm sharing a book with you about surrounding yourself with good people, understanding others by their associations, and learning when and how to let go. Earlier, I admitted I was just as much of a knucklehead as the others at Denny's. Perhaps you agree.

I drove away alone from Denny's that night for the second time, this time $100 lighter, guiltier, and with The Cure playing on the radio.

Pause, Reflect, Prepare[8]

As we conclude our examination of the profound impact our surroundings have on personal and professional growth, it's essential to summarize the key insights. Throughout "Walk with the Wise," we've emphasized the transformative power of our social circles, highlighting the necessity of surrounding ourselves with wise, inspiring individuals. This section showed how positive relationships can propel us forward, while negative ones can significantly hinder our progress.

In "Recognizing the Fruit," we sharpened our skills in discernment, learning to assess the character and actions of those around us based on their deeds rather than their words alone. This critical analysis is essential for making informed decisions about which relationships to nurture and which to reconsider. Additionally, this section stressed the importance of introspection to ensure our actions reflect our values and have a positive influence on others.

---

[8] "Pause, Reflect, Prepare" is inspired by the Hebrew word "Selah," used frequently in the Book of Psalms. Traditionally, Selah is interpreted as an instruction to pause and reflect, often suggesting a break in the song or psalm for thoughtful contemplation. This adaptation emphasizes the importance of pausing to consider the lessons learned, reflecting on their deeper meanings, and preparing to apply these insights effectively in life.

“Pruning for Growth” tackled the difficult, yet necessary task of ending relationships that no longer contribute to our well-being. Like removing a broken branch that no longer bears fruit, strategically severing unproductive or toxic relationships is essential for our health and renewal. This process involves letting go to make room for more supportive and enriching connections. We discussed methods for ending relationships with respect and ethics while also encouraging the development of new, beneficial ties.

Every person you encounter with is in fact a signpost. Pause, reflect, prepare.

Afterword

Going Far, Not Fast

As I reflect on the creation of this book, it's impossible not to draw parallels to the legendary voyage of Jason and the Argonauts in their quest for the Golden Fleece. Just as Jason did not undertake his quest alone but assembled a diverse crew, each with unique talents and strengths, I, too, recognized the importance of collaboration in crafting a work that delves deep into the intricacies of human relationships and personal growth.

Jason's selection of his crew for the Argo was a tale of strategic alliance; he chose individuals not only for their physical prowess but also for their wisdom, courage, and various other skills essential to overcoming the myriad challenges they faced. This approach resonates deeply with the process I embraced in writing this book, especially given the involvement of my children, Aaron and Syd. Their contributions have been indispensable, reflecting not only their intellectual and academic capabilities but also their profound understanding of the book's core themes.

This project was significantly shaped by my prior writing experiences. When I wrote my first book, the reaction from my children was unexpectedly subdued, marked by about 60 days of silence. My son, true to his nature, kept his thoughts to himself, wary of critiquing the work of someone he holds in high esteem—his father. He showed mature discretion, allowing the topic of the book to emerge organically in our discussions, rather than forcing his opinions upon me.

My daughter's reaction, however, was markedly different. She challenged me directly, questioning why I had not sought their input during the writing process. Her words, a blend of assertion and kindness, sparked a realization in me. I explained to her that just as they had achieved their own successes largely independently, I had initially taken a similar approach to my writing. However, I acknowledged the value that their perspectives could bring, mirroring the life lessons I aimed to impart—taking initiative and then seeking feedback.

This book represents a departure from the "take initiative and then seek feedback" approach. Recognizing the value of collaborative insight, especially from those closest to me, became a foundational pillar in the writing process. Just as Jason needed his Argonauts, I needed my most trusted advisors—my children. Their involvement ensured that the book not only benefited from their structural, aesthetic, content, and ethical critiques but also embodied a familial collaboration that enhanced its depth and relevance.

In the Spring of 2024, I officially invited Aaron and Syd to join the project. Their involvement brought fresh perspectives essential for refining the book's message. Their critiques and suggestions helped identify areas needing more depth or clarity, ensuring that the book would resonate well with its intended audience.

The concept of not going it alone, emphasized throughout the book, mirrors the very process of its creation. This work is not just a reflection of my thoughts but a synthesis of collective wisdom and familial effort. It's a testament to the power of surrounding oneself with the right people, both in life and in specific endeavors like writing this book.

Thus, as you read through these pages, understand that it is more than just a guide; it's a narrative enriched with collective intelligence and shared experiences. The principles laid out in the chapters are not merely theoretical but are supported by real-life applications, as demonstrated by the way this book was brought to fruition.

And...

As this book draws to a close, I want to share the deep-seated inspiration behind its creation and my life's approach. This inspiration is rooted in a practice I've refined throughout my life, through navigating challenging relationships and various life circumstances. My path has been marked by both trophies and scars—proof of my developed keenness to the environments I find myself in.

The impulse to write this book sprang from a desire to share how I assess whether I'm in the right place, with the right people, or if it's time to move on. This discernment has been steered by three biblical verses that have profoundly shaped my views and actions:

1. "Walk with the wise and become wise, for a companion of fools suffers harm."[9]
2. "By their fruit you will recognize them."[10]
3. "He cuts off every branch in me that bears no fruit, while every branch that does bear fruit he prunes[11] so that it will be even more fruitful."[12]

---

[9] Proverbs 13:20 (NIV)
[10] Matthew 7:16 (NIV)
[11] The Greek for he prunes also means he cleans.
[12] John 15:2 (NIV)

While I aim to avoid turning this epilogue into a sermon, it's essential to recognize how these verses have deeply influenced the content and spirit of this book.

I have often found myself in the company of questionable characters, and it's important to realize that my presence in those situations was always a choice—my choice. Denny's was my choice. As it was also my choice to disconnect from the Denny's cast. The primary message I wish to impart is clear: **You are precisely where you've chosen to be; the responsibility is yours alone**. Whether reflecting, "I had no business being there," or affirming, "I'm in the right place at the right time," it's essential to accept that these circumstances stem from intentional decisions.

A Chinese proverb eloquently states: The man who blames others has a long way to go. The man who blames himself is halfway there. The man who blames no one has already arrived.

In the preceding pages, I've counted at least 30 questions for you to ponder as you absorb the insights shared. However, among these inquiries, one overarching question stands out—the very first one from the front cover: "What am I doing here?" Take a moment now (literally) to ask yourself: "What am I doing here?" As the author, I'm not just curious about how the information impacts your thoughts; I'm intrigued by the internal and external environment in which you consume this book. "What am I doing here?" is a question that isn't solely about your physical presence in a place or situation but also about your purpose, your values, and the markers guiding your path. Look about you, not just with keen observation but with deep introspection. Read the signposts of wisdom, of caution, of opportunity, and of growth. Embrace the steps you take in the direction of self-discovery and intentional relationships, for in answering this question, you shed light on the path to a more purposeful life.

One more thing

As we conclude, I invite you to explore my previous work, *What Are You Looking At?*, focused on recognizing your audience. You've just completed *What Am I Doing Here?*, which builds upon its predecessor. Anticipate my next book, *What Was I Thinking?*, set for release in 2025. These three works reflect the pivotal questions that have guided much of my adult life, aiding me in better recognizing my audience, surrounding myself with supportive individuals, and crafting effective decision-making processes.

Enjoy the interconnectedness of these works, discover the easter eggs that link them, and stay tuned for more insights into making sound life choices.

About the Author

Adam J. San Juan is a passionate advocate for personal growth and strategic relationship management. With a deep understanding of how social connections and environments impact our personal and professional success, Adam has dedicated his career to helping others navigate these complexities.

Drawing from a wealth of diverse experiences, including a defining dine-and-dash dilemma at a Denny's Restaurant in Waukegan, IL, Adam has developed a unique perspective on the power of relationships and personal development. This incident, which profoundly tested his principles and decision-making, serves as one of the many "trophies and scars" that inform his approach to strategic relationship management.

In his latest work, "What Am I Doing Here? A Guide to the Unseen Influence of Your Surroundings," Adam builds on the insights from his first book, "What Are You Looking At? The Impact of Answering and How It Changes Everything." He shares practical strategies for assessing and managing the relationships and influences that shape our lives. His storytelling, enriched with research-backed insights and practical tools, makes this book an essential resource for anyone looking to foster positive relationships and achieve personal growth.

Driven by a commitment to the transformative power of understanding and managing unseen influences, Adam's writing and speaking engagements aim to empower readers and listeners. He invites you to join him on this path of discovery and transformation, leveraging the lessons within these pages to enrich your personal and professional life.

Acknowledgements

In writing "What Am I Doing Here?," I have explored the profound impact that our surroundings and relationships have on our personal growth and success. This book emphasizes the importance of surrounding oneself with positive influences, nurturing supportive relationships, and creating environments that foster growth and well-being. These concepts resonate deeply with the experiences my children have had through their participation in various sports teams.

I would like to extend my heartfelt gratitude to all the coaches who have ever guided my children. Your unwavering dedication to their development, both on and off the field, has been instrumental in shaping their character and success. Your commitment to bringing together groups of excellent individuals, united by a common goal, exemplifies the very essence of positive influence and collective effort.

Thank you for your tireless work, your guidance, and your ability to inspire excellence. Your contributions have not only impacted my children's lives but have also demonstrated the power of a supportive and growth-oriented environment, a central theme of this book.

Bill Larges

Bob Young

Brian Wolschlager

Casey Guntzviller

Chris Lawler

Chris Soltesz

Dan Ristau

David Keska

David Walczyk

DeAnn Allen

Joe Abraham

John Hrit

Karen Stachowski

Kevin Zurro

Kyle Gross

Marty Lowney

Michael Baum

Michael Goldberg

Michael Wilner

Mr. Mende

Nick Michniacki

Patty Nessell

Randy Hudson

Russ Holton

Scott Ampe

Steve Spickard

Wayne Probst

Recommended Resources

These ten books offer a range of insights and strategies that align well with the themes of personal development and relationship management in "What Am I Doing Here: A Guide to the Unseen Influence of Your Surrounding", providing you with a comprehensive toolkit for navigating their social and professional circles effectively.

Stephen R. Covey, "The 7 Habits of Highly Effective People", 1989

Covey's book delves into habits like proactivity and seeking mutual benefit, which are foundational in forming and sustaining relationships that are both supportive and conducive to mutual personal growth. His principles encourage developing a synergistic environment, perfect for those looking to foster a productive and positive social circle.

Dale Carnegie, “How to Win Friends and Influence People”, 1936

Carnegie provides timeless strategies on understanding people, winning them over, and influencing their behavior in a positive way, which is essential for building a supportive network. His techniques are geared towards creating empathetic and genuine interactions that can help build a foundation of trust and collaboration in any relationship.

Brené Brown, “Daring Greatly”, 2012

Brown’s examination of vulnerability in leadership and relationships offers profound insights into how showing up authentically and encouraging the same in others can deepen connections and foster an environment of growth and trust. Her examples serve as a practical guide to applying these principles in everyday life.

Carol S. Dweck, “Mindset: The New Psychology of Success”, 2006

Dweck’s distinction between fixed and growth mindsets helps in assessing the potential for personal and mutual development in relationships. Understanding these mindsets allows you to identify whether individuals view challenges as opportunities for growth, which is essential in nurturing productive and enriching interactions.

Henry Cloud and John Townsend, "Boundaries", 1992

This book is critical for understanding how and when to say no, and how to establish limits that preserve your energy and promote your well-being. The authors offer practical advice on managing interactions that drain resources or detract from personal growth, aligning perfectly with the concept of pruning in relationships.

Henry Cloud, "The Power of the Other", 2016

Cloud discusses the significant impact that others have on our performance and how the right connections can dramatically improve one's life. His examples and strategies demonstrate the importance of choosing relationships that truly drive personal advancement.

Robert B. Cialdini, "Influence: The Psychology of Persuasion", 1984

Understanding the principles of persuasion Cialdini outlines helps in discerning how you are being influenced by those around you, and also how you can ethically influence others for mutual benefit, reinforcing positive group dynamics and personal growth.

M. Scott Peck, "The Road Less Traveled", 1978

Peck addresses the less conventional, often more challenging paths to personal growth that require significant self-discipline and the courage to confront painful truths, paralleling the pruning process in personal relationships and individual development.

Daniel Goleman, "Emotional Intelligence", 1995

Goleman's examination of emotional intelligence offers tools for better understanding and managing interpersonal relationships, equipping you with the skills to assess emotional maturity and self-awareness in others, which are fundamental for sustainable and constructive relationships.

James Clear, "Atomic Habits", 2018

Clear provides structured methods for forming good habits and breaking bad ones, which can be applied to developing and maintaining healthy relationships. His focus on small changes for massive outcomes helps in cultivating environments that nurture both personal and collective growth.

Made in the USA
Monee, IL
30 December 2024

efdb39f8-f29c-4a7f-babe-9d048c54b5c3R01